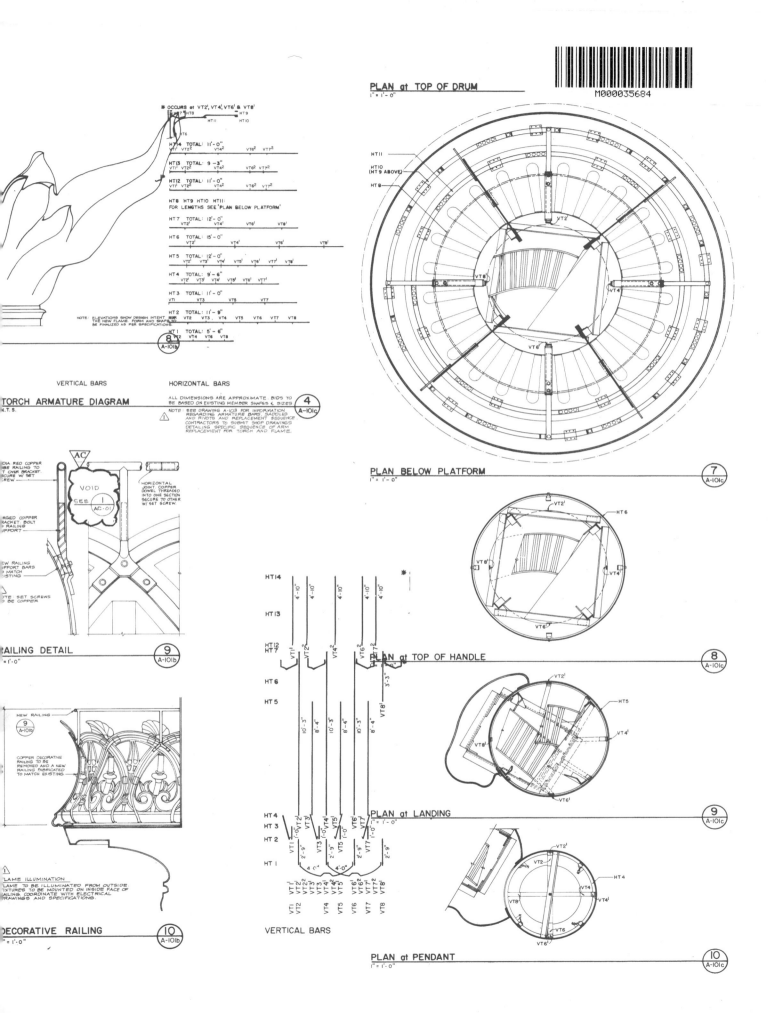

PLAN at TOP OF DRUM
1" = 1'-0"

* OCCURS at VT2', VT4', VT6' & VT8'

HT14 TOTAL: 11'-0"
HT13 TOTAL: 9'-3"
HT12 TOTAL: 11'-0"
HT8 HT9 HT10 HT11:
FOR LENGTHS SEE 'PLAN BELOW PLATFORM'
HT7 TOTAL: 12'-0"
HT6 TOTAL: 15'-0"
HT5 TOTAL: 12'-0"
HT4 TOTAL: 9'-6"
HT3 TOTAL: 11'-0"
HT2 TOTAL: 11'-9"
HT1 TOTAL: 5'-6"

NOTE: ELEVATIONS SHOW DESIGN INTENT FOR THE NEW FLAME. FORM AND SHAPE TO BE FINALIZED AS PER SPECIFICATIONS.

VERTICAL BARS   HORIZONTAL BARS

TORCH ARMATURE DIAGRAM
N.T.S.

ALL DIMENSIONS ARE APPROXIMATE. BIDS TO BE BASED ON EXISTING MEMBER SHAPES & SIZES

4
A-101c

NOTE: SEE DRAWING A-103 FOR INFORMATION REGARDING ARMATURE BARS, SADDLES AND RIVETS AND REPLACEMENT SEQUENCE. CONTRACTORS TO SUBMIT SHOP DRAWINGS DETAILING SPECIFIC SEQUENCE OF ARM REPLACEMENT FOR TORCH AND FLAME.

VOID
SEE 1 AC-01

HORIZONTAL JOINT COPPER DOWEL THREADED INTO ONE SECTION SECURE TO OTHER W/ SET SCREW.

RAILING DETAIL
9
A-101b

NEW RAILING

9
A-101b

COPPER DECORATIVE RAILING TO BE REMOVED AND A NEW RAILING FABRICATED TO MATCH EXISTING.

FLAME ILLUMINATION
FLAME TO BE ILLUMINATED FROM OUTSIDE. FIXTURES TO BE MOUNTED ON INSIDE FACE OF RAILING. COORDINATE WITH ELECTRICAL DRAWINGS AND SPECIFICATIONS.

DECORATIVE RAILING
10
A-101b

PLAN BELOW PLATFORM
1" = 1'-0"
7
A-101c

PLAN at TOP OF HANDLE
8
A-101c

HT14
HT13
HT12
HT7
HT6
HT5
HT4
HT3
HT2
HT1

VERTICAL BARS

PLAN at LANDING
1" = 1'-0"
9
A-101c

PLAN at PENDANT
1" = 1'-0"
10
A-101c

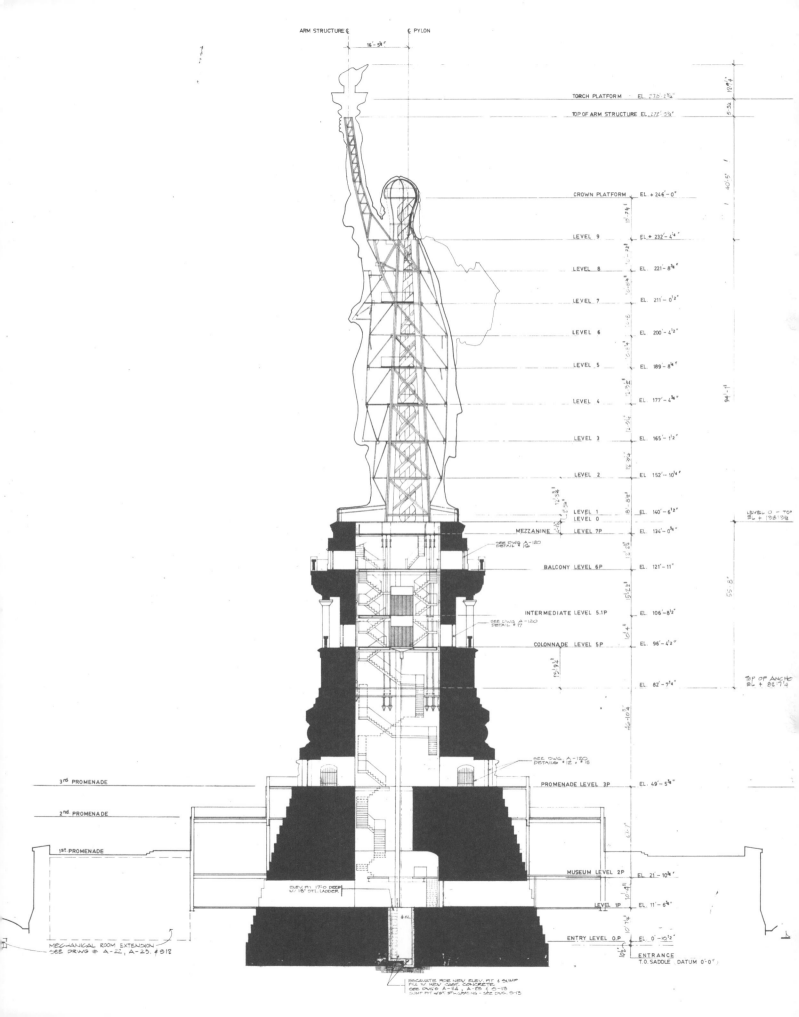

ARM STRUCTURE ₵   ₵ PYLON

16'-5¼"

TORCH PLATFORM   EL. 278'-2⅝"

TOP OF ARM STRUCTURE EL. 272'-2¾"

CROWN PLATFORM   EL. +246'-0"

LEVEL 9   EL. +232'-4¼"

LEVEL 8   EL. 221'-8¾"

LEVEL 7   EL. 211'-0½"

LEVEL 6   EL. 200'-4½"

LEVEL 5   EL. 189'-8¼"

LEVEL 4   EL. 177'-4¾"

LEVEL 3   EL. 165'-1½"

LEVEL 2   EL. 152'-10¼"

LEVEL 1   EL. 140'-6½"
LEVEL 0   LEVEL 0 - TOP
                               EL. + 138'-3⅜"

MEZZANINE   LEVEL 7P   EL. 134'-0¾"

SEE DWG A-120
DETAIL # 16

BALCONY LEVEL 6P   EL. 121'-11"

INTERMEDIATE LEVEL 5.1P   EL. 106'-8½"

SEE DWG A-120
DETAIL # 17

COLONNADE LEVEL 5P   EL. 96'-4½"

EL. 82'-7¼"   TOP OF ANCH.
              EL. + 82'-7¼"

SEE DWG. A-120
DETAILS # 12 & 15

3rd PROMENADE

PROMENADE LEVEL 3P   EL. 49'-5¾"

2nd PROMENADE

1st PROMENADE

MUSEUM LEVEL 2P   EL. 21'-10¾"

ELEV. PIT 17'-0 DEEP
W/ 18' STL. LADDER

LEVEL 1P   EL. 11'-6¾"

MECHANICAL ROOM EXTENSION
SEE DRWG # A-21, A-23, & B12

ENTRY LEVEL 0.P   EL. 0'-10½"

ENTRANCE
T.O. SADDLE DATUM 0'-0"

EXCAVATE FOR NEW ELEV. PIT & SUMP
FILL W/ NEW OBT. CONCRETE
SEE DWG A-114, A-83 & 5-13
SUMP PIT W/8" STL. GRATING - SEE DWG. S-13

The Statue of Liberty

The Monumental Dream

The Statue of Liberty

Liberty

text by
Robert Belot

preface by
Diane von Furstenberg

The Monumental Dream

RIZZOLI
NEW YORK

New York Paris London Milan

Dedicated to all people throughout the world
who have continually given whatever they could afford
to help the Statue of Liberty: from its initial creation
and building the pedestal in the 1880s, to contributing
to the 1986 centennial restoration, to supporting the
construction of the Statue of Liberty Museum in 2019.

Preface

I was a little girl living in Belgium when I saw the Statue of Liberty for the first time. It was on a postcard my parents sent me from their trip to New York. It was one of those happy customized postcards that featured Lady Liberty next to a photo of smiling tourists, in this case my parents. I not only marveled at the magnitude of the Statue, but also immediately associated her with happiness and adventure. My own desire to visit America started then. The second time I saw her, she was real and bigger than life. It was October 1969, at six in the morning. I was on board the large Italian ship *Raffaello*, which had just crossed the Atlantic Ocean, and there she was, welcoming me to a new horizon and a new beginning. I had just married. I was expecting a child and starting a new life in America. Like millions before me, the Statue of Liberty was the first thing I saw as I sailed into Manhattan. And like millions before me, just the sight of her meant that my dream of building a future in America had come true.

In 1986, for the Statue's centennial, and at the time of her restoration, Mayor Edward I. Koch distributed eighty-seven Liberty Award medals to people who had immigrated and contributed to the city of New York. Amongst very distinguished scholars, scientists, and artists such as Itzhak Perlman, Mikhail Baryshnikov, and Milos Forman, all having achieved the American Dream, here I was, the only one representing Belgium. Belgium, my native country, is actually what paved the way to my involvement with Lady Liberty. It was from Antwerp that the famous Red Star Line's transatlantic ships set sail to America. They were luxury liners, but also brought refugees, amongst them Albert Einstein. It was also in Antwerp, at the opening of the Red Star Line Museum in 2013, that I met Stephen A. Briganti. Stephen Briganti is the president and CEO of The Statue of Liberty-Ellis Island Foundation, Inc., and a passionate visionary whose organization, since 1982, has enhanced both Ellis and Liberty Islands with the Statue's restoration and celebration of her centennial, new and expanded museums, and a center that holds records of arrival through the Port of New York from 1820 to 1957. Stephen pursued me for two years until I joined the Foundation's prestigious board of directors. My role? To help raise the funds to build the new Statue of Liberty Museum on her island.

This is when I became the "Godmother" of the Statue, and embarked on the most extraordinary adventure. It has taken me through a fascinating journey into the history of France and America, their friendship and respect, and into the making of dreams. I learned of Édouard de Laboulaye, who first proposed the idea of a gift from the people of France to the people of America, and Frédéric-Auguste Bartholdi, the ambitious sculptor who dreamt of building the largest statue in the world. I discovered the meaning of what they set out to do: celebrate the help that France had given the United States during the Revolutionary War and reaffirm their respect for the values of the American Constitution and its ideals of freedom and democracy. The more I learned about the Statue—about conceiving her, raising the money from the people of France for building her, transporting her, raising the funds from the people of America for her pedestal—the more I read about all the illustrious people like Gustave Eiffel, Victor Hugo, and Joseph Pulitzer who fought for her existence, and the people who looked up to her as they pursued their own goals and dreams, the more seduced and fascinated I became.

Lady Liberty belongs to everyone. Like the sun, she warms us all. Her iconic image adorns postcards, stamps, T-shirts, and toys. She is the symbol of freedom, hope, inclusiveness. She embodies America and all of its values. She is the American Dream.

My journey with the Statue has been one of true discovery. Of all the people I met and interviewed about Lady Liberty, the most impressive was the French historian Robert Belot. Robert spent years of his life working on an extensive biography of Bartholdi. Over dinner at my place, Robert kindly agreed to write the text for this book and, thanks to Rizzoli, The Statue of Liberty-Ellis Island Foundation, the National Park Service, and Diego Marini, who designed it, this beautiful book came together in record time!

The Statue of Liberty is not just a magnificent monument, a destination, and a unique symbol of the history of immigration and the values of tolerance; I also discovered that she truly has the power to make things happen. She has a magic torch!

I want to thank Edwin Schlossberg, who designed the museum experience, for helping me to conceive the donor wall; artist Anh Duong for sculpting the stars; and all of the donors for their incredible generosity.

It has been a privilege to serve the board of The Statue of Liberty-Ellis Island Foundation. I hope to continue to do so for a long time.

— Diane von Furstenberg

Foreword

In 1886, sculptor Frédéric-Auguste Bartholdi gave form to our most powerful symbol of freedom—*Liberty Enlightening the World*. A century later, with the Statue of Liberty approaching her centennial and in need of major restoration, President Reagan asked Lee Iacocca to lead a national effort to raise funds from the American people and manage the entire effort to give the Lady a facelift. And who better? Lee was America's most famous and successful businessman, the son of Ellis Island immigrants, and the epitome of achieving the American Dream.

As a first-generation American, whose mother and all four grandparents first set foot on U.S. soil at Ellis Island, it was the honor of my life to be selected by Mr. Iacocca to assist in this historic endeavor, leading The Statue of Liberty-Ellis Island Foundation, Inc. I realized early on we weren't just restoring buildings or monuments. The Statue and Ellis Island resonate in people's hearts and minds around the world, and as living symbols of freedom, hope, opportunity, and welcome.

It's been a long journey for the Foundation, which has raised nearly $1 billion, all from private, non-governmental donations. First, we worked with our partner the U.S. Department of the Interior/National Park Service to restore Lady Liberty for her 1986 centennial, culminating in the "Liberty Weekend" celebration that was seen by 1.5 billion people around the world.

Then we focused on Ellis Island, restoring America's largest immigration station, which welcomed over twelve million people to a new life. In 1990, restoration of the Main Registry Building became the beginning of what is now the Ellis Island National Museum of Immigration, which chronicles American arrival from the 1550s through today. The Foundation also established The American Immigrant Wall of Honor as a tribute to family heritage, the American Family Immigration History Center for researching records of family arrival in America, and the expansive Peopling of America Center.

Security restrictions of the post-9/11 era returned us to Liberty Island. Only 20 percent of the island's 4.5 million annual visitors were allowed into the monument and galleries, leaving 80 percent of the visitors without any museum experience. A freestanding museum, updated and expanded, was needed. But a dynamic campaign leader was crucial. Lee Iacocca had been that person for us in the 1980s and '90s. How about a powerful woman, preferably an immigrant, who had experienced the American Dream? Enter Diane von Furstenberg, who became Lady Liberty's godmother and the inspirational leader of our fundraising campaign.

I couldn't be more grateful to Diane for the incomparable job she has done in helping make this beautiful museum a reality. Diane's name now joins those of Édouard de Laboulaye, Frédéric-Auguste Bartholdi, Gustave Eiffel, Joseph Pulitzer, Presidents Grover Cleveland, Franklin D. Roosevelt, and Ronald Reagan, François Mitterrand, and Lee Iacocca for their important contributions to the Statue of Liberty's rich and ongoing history.

I am also deeply grateful to our board and, of course, the American people, who never flagged in their generous support of these two beloved monuments, and to the thousands of people who worked on these projects over the years. We can all take pride in the roles we played in Keeping Lady Liberty's Torch Lit and preserving the stories of Ellis Island and the American immigration experience.

But that work is far from done. The story of freedom in our nation, and throughout the world, is ever evolving. It deserves our ongoing reflection and demands to be shared if we are to safeguard it. Let the new Statue of Liberty Museum serve as inspiration.

— Stephen A. Briganti
President & Chief Executive Officer
The Statue of Liberty-Ellis Island
Foundation, Inc.

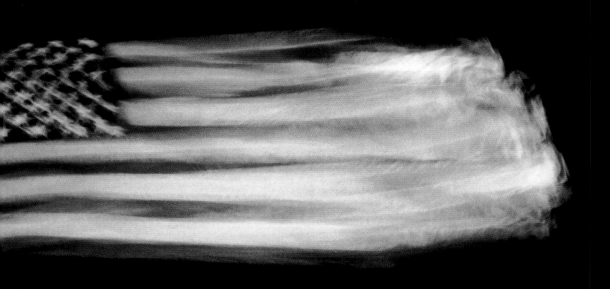

First published in the United States of America
in 2019 by Rizzoli Electa,
a division of Rizzoli International Publications, Inc.
300 Park Avenue South
New York, NY 10010
www.rizzoliusa.com

Design by **YummyColours**
Text by **Robert J.L. Belot**

For Rizzoli Electa
Charles Miers, *Publisher*
Margaret Rennolds Chace, *Associate Publisher*
James O. Muschett, *Associate Publisher and Project Manager*
Elizabeth Smith, *Editor*

For The Statue of Liberty–Ellis Island Foundation, Inc.
Stephen A. Briganti, *President and Chief Executive Officer*
Richard P. Flood, *Vice President, Chief Advancement Officer*
Suzanne Mannion, *Director of Public Affairs*
Nadia Lee, *Director of Fundraising & Marketing*
Elizabeth Oravetz, *Manager, Public Relations*
Peg Zitko, *Communications Consultant*

For the National Park Service,
Statue of Liberty National Monument and Ellis Island
John Piltzecker, *Superintendent*
John Hnedak, D*eputy Superintendent*
Diana Pardue, *Chief, Museum Services Division*
Barry Moreno, *Bob Hope Memorial Library*

Front and back cover photography by Jake Rajs

Library of Congress Control Number: 2019933531
ISBN: 978-0-8478-6730-1 (hardcover)
ISBN: 978-0-8478-6729-5 (paperback)
2019 2020 2021 2022 / 10 9 8 7 6 5 4 3 2 1
Printed in China

The Statue of Liberty-Ellis Island Foundation, Inc. is a non-profit organization established in 1982 to raise funds for and oversee the historic restoration and preservation of the Statue of Liberty and Ellis Island.
The Foundation's collaboration with the U.S. Department of the Interior/National Park Service is one of the most successful public-private partnership in U.S. history, with the Foundation raising nearly $1 billion from the American people and supporters from around the world.
In addition to restoring the monuments, the Foundation conceptualized, created and constructed museums on both islands, including the Statue of Liberty Museum opened in 2019, as well as The American Immigrant Wall of Honor, the American Family Immigration History Center, and The Peopling of America Center, which in 2015 transformed the museum on Ellis Island into the Ellis Island National Museum of Immigration. The organization's endowment has funded over 250 additional projects that support these national treasures.
For more information, and to contribute, please visit: **libertyellisfoundation.org**

Contents

"I Found an Admirable Location."

Viewed from the rooftop platform of Liberty Island's new museum, the Statue of Liberty stands before the city of New York as if it has always stood on that very spot. The Statue blends so harmoniously with the urban landscape that the city and port seem to have been designed by it and for it. As one member of the French delegation said during the Statue's 1886 dedication, "The island was created for Bartholdi's statue rather than the statue for the island."

The sculptor Frédéric-Auguste Bartholdi reinvented this island and, in doing so, reinvented the symbolic entry to the city and the nation. He created a landscape that is profoundly resonant—the monument attracts more than four million visitors each year.

The Statue is more than a statue; it is a central element in the scenography of a site that merges land and sea, culture and nature, a city and the world.

Bartholdi wasn't attached to the colossal for its own sake. A pioneering practitioner of what today is called Land art, he strove to break with the rigid expectations of classical statuary art in which the monument is assigned the role of an autonomous object.

His concept was instead a Lady Liberty overlooking the city from a great height, taller than any building in New York at the time—creating a view from the Statue's grand perspective in which this city was the pinnacle of the world.

BEDLOE'S ISLAND BEFORE THE ERECTION OF STATUE.

The Statue of Liberty transforms nature—the island—into a cultural symbol. It transfigures a harbor into a lasting symbol of civilization. It was designed to accentuate not only an oceanic vastness but also the whole world that its torch intends to illuminate.

In 1886, the date of her inauguration, Lady Liberty looked at the world; today it's the world who looks upon her. To achieve this required the master stroke of an artist.

It is June 1871. France has just lost a devastating war against Prussia. Alsace, where Bartholdi was born, is now under German rule. Paris, where Bartholdi lives, is putting itself back together after the failed revolution of the Paris Commune. Disappointed in France, the idealistic Bartholdi is searching for a new source of inspiration, a new world. He dreams of America.

On June 10, 1871, in Brest, Bartholdi boards the *Eugène Pereire*, of the French Line, which directly connects France to the United States. The trip proves to be rougher than expected. Wind blows and disturbs dinners. When he's not seasick, he reads, plays chess, learns English, chats with fellow travelers, and observes the water's movement and the changes of the sky.

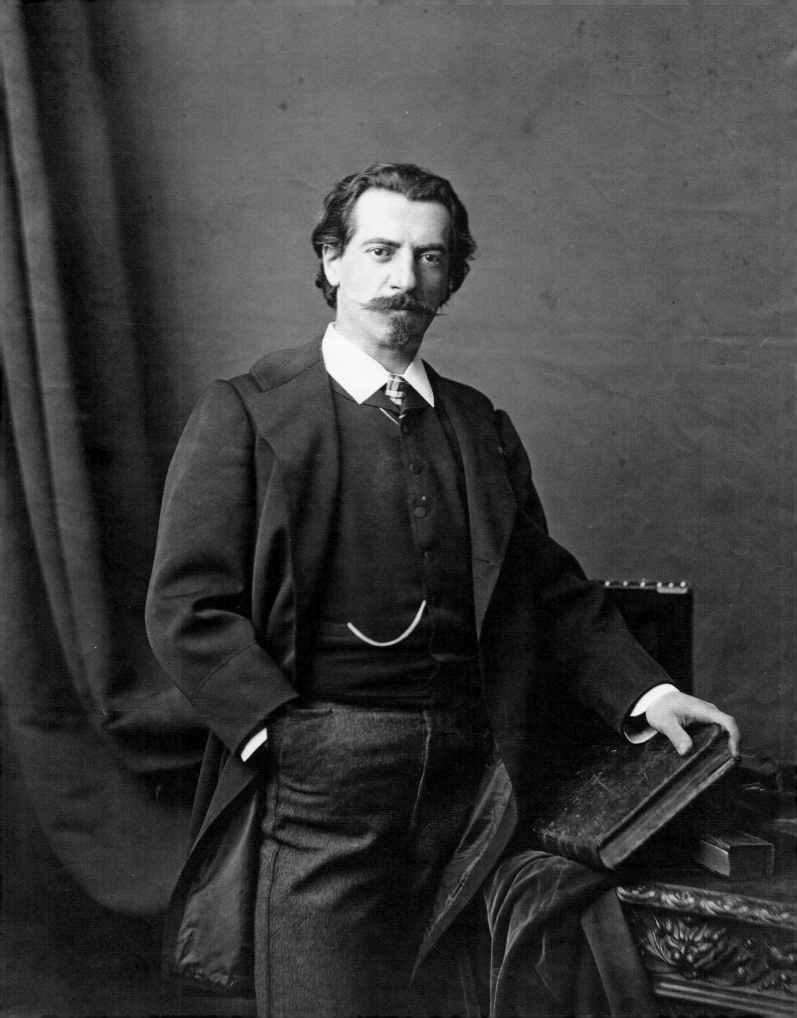

Vendredi 9. Arrivé à Rennes passé la
matinée avec la famille Simon, vu
le préfet Barthélemy (du Cercle) qui m'a
fait demander départ à 3 h. - arrivé
à Brest minuit. L'école de Nantes a
mal parti

Samedi 10 Visité Brest, aspect général
pont tournant sont le plus remarquable
embarqués à 1 h. On ne part qu'à
5 h. on se met à table après dîner
nous voyons disparaître la côte!!

Dimanche 11 Mauvais temps.

Lundi 12 très mauvais avarie

Mardi 13 médiocre

Mercredi 14 un peu de répit, nous
nous remettons un peu j'ai été très
découragé ces 3 jours

Jeudi 15 temps passable

Vendredi 16 — beau

Samedi 17 — brouillards

Dimanche 18 beau puis brouillard

Lundi 19 médiocre, pluie

Mardi 20 passable brouillards

Mercredi 21 En vue de la terre à 4 h.
du matin. Nous entrons et restons
en rade, aspect merveilleux du
mouvement d'animation. Je prends
congé de quelques compagnons de route

"And today you see telegraphs in the form of spiders' webs, hundreds of newspapers; the whistles of boats and railroads create a continuous Aeolian harp music; the smoke darkens the sky; you see a huge population run, hurried by the colic of business. You don't understand how all of that could be created in such little time. It's marvelous..."

— Frédéric-Auguste Bartholdi

On June 21, in the morning, his dream becomes a reality. With a feeling of excited liberation, Bartholdi spots New York's silhouette. In the diary that he'll keep throughout this visit, he notes:

Sight of land at 4:00 in the morning. We enter the harbor. Marvelous feeling of movement, animation. I take leave of several traveling companions. Disembarkation. Finicky customs. . . . The cars, buses, potholed cobblestones, railways, poles, flags, goods, and signs. I go to Henri Maillard's, Broadway 619, a fellow traveler. I prefer that to large inns. Send a telegram to Mother and some letters. I run to get a first glance at my project. The Battery, Central Park, the island. Then a bath and rest.

Bartholdi speaks about "his project," which will be his obsession throughout this trip. His singular idea of a monument commemorating the close relationship between France and the United States is in its nascent stage—this trip will determine if it would even be welcome in the United States.

"The small island appears to be the ideal spot."

— Frédéric-Auguste Bartholdi

Newly arrived at his hotel, the sculptor feels the need to examine a site that he spotted from the boat, Bedloe's Island, which, at that time, was a military fort.

With surprising foresight, he immediately recognizes that this could be the location to host his work. The very next day, he is on the ferry to Staten Island. He again observes the harbor and notes in his diary: "The small island appears to be the ideal spot." This powerful intuition stays with him. It has taken Bartholdi only two days to identify the place where he will install the most renowned monument in the world. But while the traveler strongly believes in his "project," he is conscious of the audacious nature of this endeavor and recommends total discretion to his mother: "If you communicate about my letters, you'll leave out that which concerns my projects. There are people who couldn't understand and to whom I'd seem extravagant."

At first New York's overall impression seems "strange" to him. He sees a "bustling of rushed people." The streets have broken cobblestones, are lined with telegraph poles and lopsided gas lamps. Rarely hosed down or swept, the streets are flanked by signs and awnings "like at a fairground" and it's not uncommon to see sidewalks cluttered with merchandise. The trees sometimes seem to "come out of caves." The buildings are "uneven." The main streets are maintained little better. He notices "very tall" homes, buildings with eight stories, and others with two. The absence of a coherent architectural style bothers this European.

But as the days go by, Bartholdi comes to appreciate this anything-is-possible city. Enamored by modernity, he raves about the transportation system, very developed and very easy to use, thanks to elevated trains, a great novelty of the time that allows for "mass transit." "The city is very big and wheels are an absolute necessity," he says. He visits Central Park and meets its creators, the landscape architects Frederick Law Olmsted and Calvert Vaux. The ensemble is very beautiful, to his eyes, well designed, "animated, elegant, clean, and well-groomed." The only disappointment: the "mediocre statues." The three men go to Brooklyn to visit Prospect Park, which, he thinks, "could offer a location" for his work.

The Statue of Liberty as seen from New York Harbor, circa 1905.

In New York, and on trips to Washington, Boston, Newport, and Philadelphia, the artist seeks out support for his monument in artistic, journalistic, and political milieus, thanks to the contacts provided by his mentor Édouard de Laboulaye, a well-known French lecturer who admires the American system of governance and who encouraged Bartholdi to make the trip. Bartholdi meets the first editor in chief of *Harper's Bazaar*, Miss Mary Louise Booth, who translated Laboulaye's works into English, among others by French writers sympathetic to the anti-slavery cause.

In the Massachusetts town of Nahant, he's invited to the home of famous poet Henry Wadsworth Longfellow, a professor at Harvard; earlier Bartholdi met his son, Ernest, during his trip to Paris. The poet, he says, "showed me the greatest cordiality and a lot of enthusiasm for the monument."

Bartholdi shows a portfolio of his works to the painter Charles Persons, director of the Harper bookstore, and to the sculptor John Quincy Adams Ward. He likes American decorative arts and visits the large furniture ateliers of the great importer Charles Cottier, at 171 Broadway. He meets with Michael Knoedler, a gallery owner on Fifth Avenue.

He also meets with several politicians, like Charles Sumner, a Republican senator from the state of Massachusetts and a prominent abolitionist. At Sumner's home, he befriends John W. Forney, founder of the influential *Philadelphia Press*, who will be a loyal supporter throughout the project. It proves to be a fortuitous meeting, because Forney introduces him to the Union League, a New York philanthropic club with 1,700 members, all of whom fought for the Union against slavery—Laboulaye has been an honorary member of this elite group of wealthy and informed individuals since 1863.

top
A reproduction of the view of New York Harbor from the steeple of Trinity Church.

bottom, left
Brooklyn ferry boat.

bottom, center
Stereograph of the Manhattan Life Insurance Building. Completed in 1894, at 348 feet it was the tallest skyscraper in New York City.

bottom, right
Elevated train line in New York City, circa 1870.

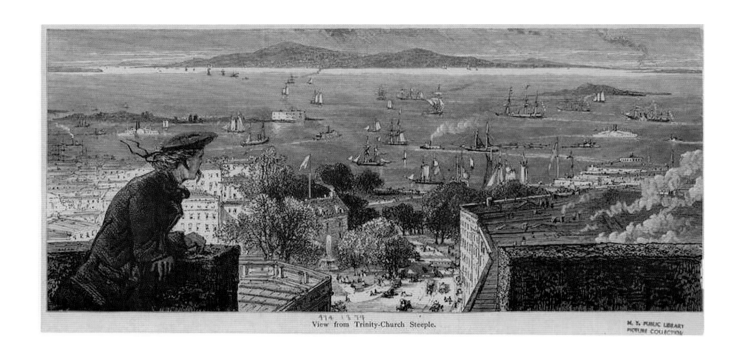

View from Trinity-Church Steeple.

N. Y. City & Vicinity.

4113.—Brooklyn Ferry Boat. Inst.

A. S. CAMPBELL, ELIZABETH, N. J.

American Views.

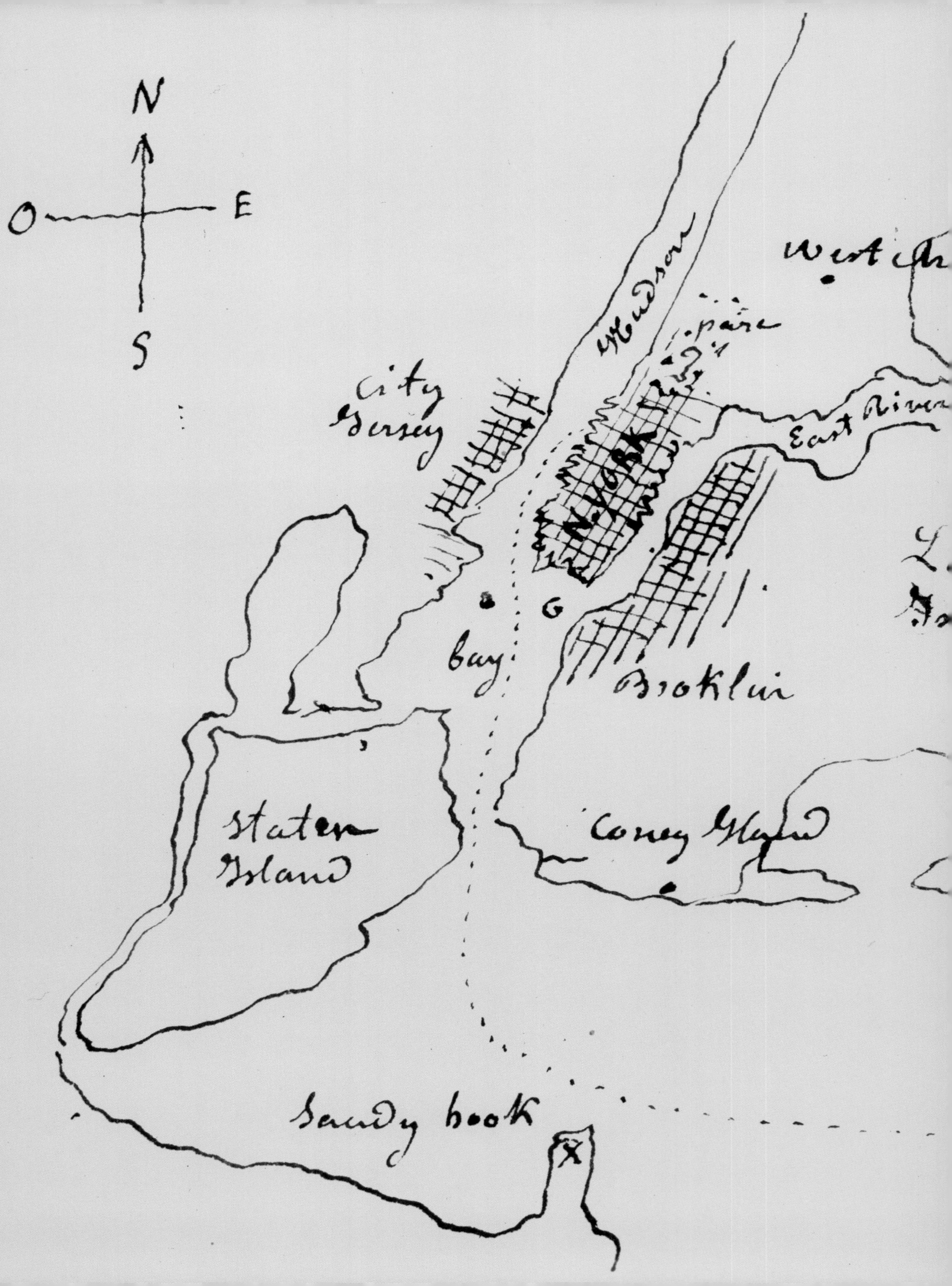
N
O
E
S
Hudson
West
City Jersey
N. YORK
East River
G
bay
Broklin
Staten Island
Coney Island
Sandy hook
X

On Tuesday, July 11, 1871, the Union League hosts a dinner in honor of Bartholdi. As a military outpost, Bedloe's Island is owned by the government, and so, one week after the dinner, still with Forney, the Frenchman meets with the president of the United States, Ulysses S. Grant. In showing the president his plans, Bartholdi notes that Grant is welcoming, with a "reserved friendliness, simple but real."

They smoke a cigar together on the veranda of Grant's summer cottage, but the president doesn't promise anything to the French artist. It's through the Union League that the sculptor is introduced to leading New York architect Richard Morris Hunt, who is well regarded for his designs of monumental public buildings. Describing him as "slightly boastful, sure of himself" in his journal, Bartholdi cannot know that one day he will be the designer of the Statue's pedestal.

Another essential encounter is with Richard Butler, who will become a trustworthy friend. This wealthy industrialist, president of the Butler Hard Rubber Company, is an art collector and involved in the creation of the Metropolitan Museum of Art, which will open its doors in 1872. Butler will eventually become the secretary of the American Committee of the Franco-American Union, an organization that will be formed in 1875 to secure funds for the Statue and pedestal and oversee their execution.

After this series of impressive meetings, Bartholdi decides to journey through the heartland of the United States, all the way to California and back—an exhausting trip in a Pullman coach drawn by a steam locomotive that he finds "extraordinary": Chicago, Omaha, Columbus, the Rocky Mountains, Salt Lake City, Sacramento, Oakland, San Francisco, Denver, Kansas City, Saint Louis, Pittsburgh . . . Bartholdi is enthralled by what he sees—the "rough beauty" of its landscape enchants him, as well as the unprecedented technical feats that have allowed travel to expand across the vast continent. Bridges, viaducts, tunnels represent, to his eyes, a "fantastic construction of boldness and ingenuity, like everything you see here." The European is impressed by the just-built Niagara Clifton Bridge connecting the United States to Canada.

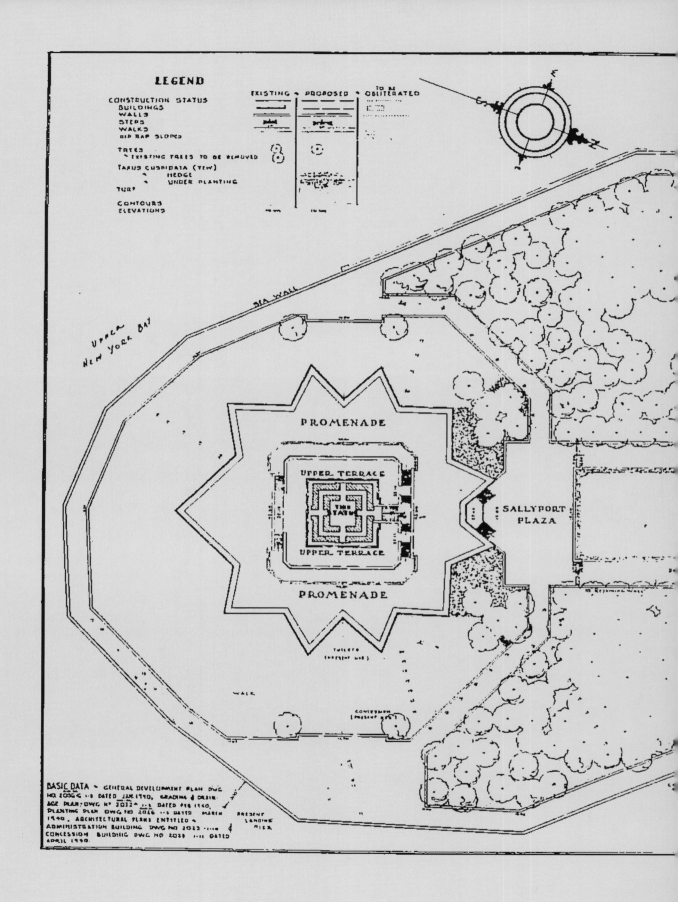

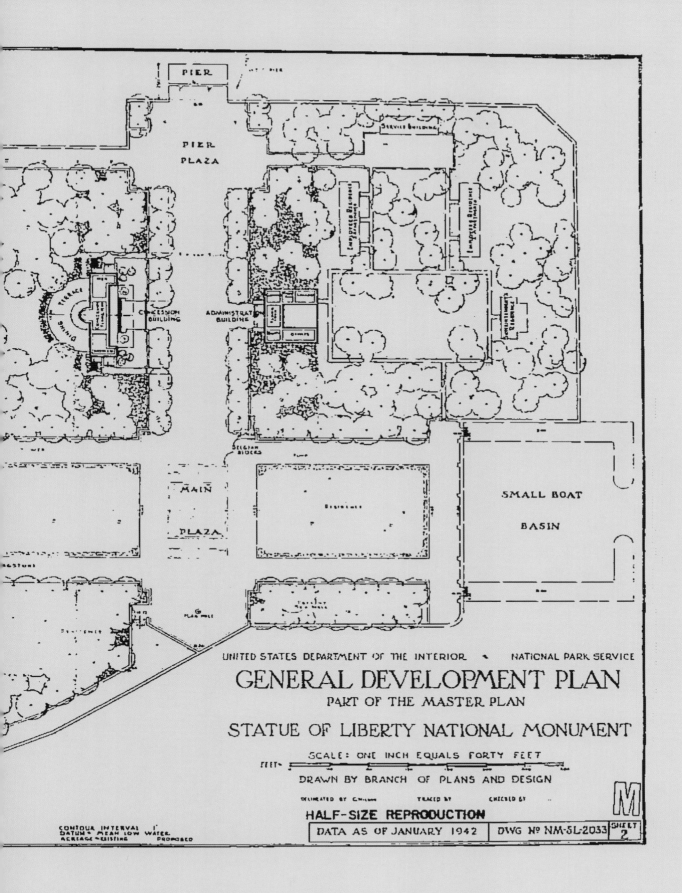

UNITED STATES DEPARTMENT OF THE INTERIOR • NATIONAL PARK SERVICE

GENERAL DEVELOPMENT PLAN
PART OF THE MASTER PLAN

STATUE OF LIBERTY NATIONAL MONUMENT

SCALE: ONE INCH EQUALS FORTY FEET

DRAWN BY BRANCH OF PLANS AND DESIGN

DELINEATED BY C.W___   TRACED BY   CHECKED BY

HALF-SIZE REPRODUCTION

| DATA AS OF JANUARY 1942 | DWG Nº NM-5L-2033 | SHEET 2 |

CONTOUR INTERVAL 1'
DATUM - MEAN LOW WATER
ACREAGE - EXISTING   PROPOSED

PIER

PIER PLAZA

SERVICE BUILDING

CONCESSION BUILDING

ADMINISTRATION BUILDING

DINING TERRACE

BELGIAN BLOCKS

MAIN PLAZA

SMALL BOAT BASIN

FLAG POLE

Bartholdi is fascinated by American cities' booming
growth, like Chicago, which had only five inhabitants in
1804 but 299,000 in 1871. "And today you see telegraphs
in the form of spiders' webs, hundreds of newspapers;
the whistles of boats and railroads create a continuous
Aeolian harp music; the smoke darkens the sky; you see
a huge population run, hurried by the colic of business.
You don't understand how all of that could be created in
such little time. It's marvelous . . ." In all of the traversed
territories, "civilization bites every day." Memories of
his trips result in numerous drawings and watercolors,
and two paintings of immense beauty: *La Californie de
jadis* (The Former California) and *La Californie nouvelle*
(New California).

His trek into the heartland of the United States ends back
in New York on September 15, 1871. Exhausted but happy,
Bartholdi revisits his project. He notes in his journal:
"Last look at the bay and Bedloe's Island. I look at it with
the same conviction as the arrival." Saturday, October 7,
1871, is its true beginning. He announces to Laboulaye,
"I found an admirable location." And he promises that
this monument will be "a work of great moral value."

"I found an admirable location."

— Frédéric-Auguste Bartholdi

"Maybe one day, bene
lantern, you will see th
that you love today; m
diminishing shadow, y
charm of her immorta
sister of justice and m
equality, of prosperity
This day, dear reader,
I confide to you go out
that pressures and pu
the path to the future.

th the glow of my

e ugliness of the idols

ybe also, beyond the

ou'll notice, in the

smile, liberty, the

rcy, the mother of

nd peace.

Édouard de Laboulaye
Paris in America, 1863

on't let the flame that

illuminate this youth

hes us by asking for

When Europe Began to Dream of the American Republic

"America, thy lot was cast by powers Happier than those of our old Continent ..."

— Johann Wolfgang von Goethe,
"To the United States," 1827

Today, the Statue of Liberty is seen as a symbol of welcome to immigrants, famously described in Emma Lazarus's poem "The New Colossus"—"Give me your tired, your poor, your huddled masses yearning to breathe free ..." But this meaning has only been attributed to the Statue since 1903, when the now-famous sonnet was inscribed onto a plaque and placed on the Statue's pedestal. The Statue embodies a concept of the United States—and the world—that goes beyond issues of immigration.

To understand Bartholdi's original intent, one must return to 1776, when the American colonies issued their Declaration of Independence from England.
This date appears in Roman numerals on the tablet that the Statue of Liberty holds in its left hand; this tablet represents the rule of law. During the eighteenth century, European intellectuals such as Voltaire, Immanuel Kant, Alexis de Tocqueville, Jean-Jacques Rousseau, and Montesquieu were writing of emancipation and political change in the service of a new democracy, the separation of powers, and the protection of individual liberties by law. Indeed, the expressions "citizen of the world" and "cosmopolitan law" are from this era. In 1776, Americans accomplished what Europeans had long dreamed of.

The Bartholdi family, Protestants from the Alsace region between France and Germany, were steeped in the culture of emancipation. Charlotte Bartholdi read to her son the writers and poets who dreamed of a universal republic, such as Johann Wolfgang von Goethe and Friedrich Schiller, the latter of whom was acquainted with Alsace and met the young Auguste's grandfather and his friend, the famous blind poet from Colmar, Conrad Pfeffel. It's through Goethe that Bartholdi first heard the United States evoked in a positive light, in his poem "To the United States": "America, thy lot was cast by powers / Happier than those of our old Continent…" As an adolescent, Bartholdi read Schiller's play *Fiesco*, which was presented as a "republican drama."
The United States had become a model of civilization, its highest principle being freedom: freedom of conscience as well as freedom to think, to publish, to travel, and to live in peace.

The concept of liberty also guided Bartholdi's teacher, the Romantic painter Ary Scheffer, who was a close friend of the Marquis de Lafayette, a Frenchman who fought by Washington's side during the Revolutionary War. One of Scheffer's works hangs in the U.S. Capitol in Washington, D.C., one of two portraits framing the Speaker's seat in the House Chamber. Opposite American painter John Vanderlyn's 1834 portrait of George Washington is a painting of a man with a haughty air, informally dressed and wearing a cape as he stands against a cloudy sky: Lafayette. Signed by Scheffer, this portrait was given to the American government in 1822.

"If a monument was ever erected in America in memory of its independence, it would seem natural to me that it be erected through a communal effort by the two nations."

— Édouard de Laboulaye

DESIGN.

A. BARTHOLDI.
Statue.

No. 11,023.   Patented Feb. 18, 1879.

LIBERTY ENLIGHTENING THE WORLD.

In Scheffer's studio, a young Bartholdi crossed paths with Scheffer's brother, Arnold, who was Lafayette's secretary. A politically active journalist and the author of a book critical of the French government, for which he was put on trial, Arnold also admired the American model of governance. In 1825 he published a *Histoire des États-Unis de l'Amérique septentrionale* (History of the United States of Northern America), which the sculptor read. It included an homage to Lafayette and his role as a "defender of the great cause of the human race, liberty." Bartholdi's presence at Scheffer's studio was with the blessing of his mother, Charlotte, who wrote in her diary on August 31, 1853: "Dined at M. Scheffer's. A magnificent dinner. Very interesting conversation. Music, painting, gardening, literature, here's a world that pleases me."

Scheffer's studio, at rue Chaptal in Paris (today the Museum of Romantic Life), was at the heart of a circle of intellectuals and artists campaigning for a liberal Europe that included composers Frédéric Chopin and Franz Liszt, historian Ernest Renan, feminist writer George Sand, and German writer Heinrich Heine. Scheffer and his reform-minded friends enthusiastically received Alexis de Tocqueville's *Democracy in America*, first published in 1835, and Scheffer viewed the republican aristocrat Lafayette as an embodiment of France's moral and military support of the Americans, a fighter for political liberties, a Freemason, and the French leader of the liberal opposition against the Restoration regime (1814–1830). Bartholdi himself showed his admiration for Lafayette with two statues of the general, one dedicated in New York City's Union Square in 1876, and one in which Lafayette is portrayed with George Washington, unveiled in 1895 at Place des États-Unis in Paris.

DEPARTMENT OF PUBLIC PARKS,
36 UNION SQUARE,
New York, 31st August, 1876.

To *Madame Bartholdi - à Colmar*

Madame SIR—You are respectfully informed that the Statue of

LAFAYETTE,

By A. BARTHOLDI, will be presented by

THE REPUBLIC OF FRANCE

TO THE

CITY OF NEW YORK,

At half-past three o'clock, in the afternoon of the 6th September, 1876, on which occasion your attendance is requested.

EDMOND BREUIL,
Consul General of France.

WILLIAM R. MARTIN,
President of the Department of Public Parks.

Please to present this note at the entrance to the seats.

M. EDOUARD LABOULAYE.

At a young age Bartholdi became familiar with the history of the United States and the values of liberty and universality; in this light, the Statue of Liberty can be viewed as part homage to Lafayette and to Scheffer, who had opened Bartholdi's eyes to what the United States represented. For the idea of a monument dedicated to liberty to take root and flourish, a man and an event were needed. The man was Édouard de Laboulaye. He was a journalist, essayist, and professor of comparative law at the Collège de France; five hundred people crowded into the lecture hall every week to hear him laud the virtues of United States' governance. An emblematic figure of French liberalism and opposition to Napoléon III, he believed U.S. democratic institutions to be the inspiration France should follow to revive its republic. His 1863 satirical novel *Paris in America*, published under the pseudonym René Lefevre, was a huge success in the States as well as France, and, in 1866, Laboulaye translated into French and annotated *Memoirs of Benjamin Franklin; Written by Himself*.

He was a member of historical societies in New York and Massachusetts, and his impressive reputation in the United States and political and cultural connections would be leveraged by Bartholdi in the years to come to gain support for his Statue of Liberty.

In 1863, an American newspaper published a profile of Laboulaye, in which he described the potential of the United States:

I am fifty-three years old; I spent my entire life working alone. Then renown came to find me. . . . Paris in America, having sold twelve thousand copies today and whose success continues, did more for my name than twenty-five years of serious work. . . . What delights me in this success is that America enjoys it more than I do. Today, it represents the ideal for all our good workers. Let us allow time to act, and we too will organize democracy.

Laboulaye admired the American people because they had "energetically conquered an unparalleled civil war" and "triumphed in the revolt without taking refuge in a dictatorship, which is always mortal to liberty." The United States was "an all-powerful democracy that only owes to itself its prosperity and magnificence," a "model" for "old Europe," which had seen eighty years of unrest and misery. And to what did Laboulaye believe the Americans owed this triumph? To their ability to distance themselves from European culture: "Immigrated [to the United States] from old Europe, they left behind royalty, nobility, the Church, centralization, permanent armies: privilege never came to them."

"Here's a world that pleases me."

— Charlotte Bartholdi

© MOLE & THOMAS
915 MEDINAH BLDG.
CHICAGO, ILL.

HUMAN STATUE OF LIBERTY
18,000 OFFICERS AND MEN
AT
CAMP DODGE, DES MOINES IA.
COL. WM. NEWMAN, COMMANDING
COL. RUSH S. WELLS, DIRECTING.

This idea struck a chord with Bartholdi. Throughout the following decade, taken with the challenge of representing the ideals of liberty and democracy on a colossal scale, the sculptor explored this idea through sketches and models. He believed the United States would be a fitting home for his colossus and shared his plan with Laboulaye.

If the man was Laboulaye, the event was the assassination of Abraham Lincoln on April 14, 1865. Much later in Bartholdi's life, he claimed that his inspiration for the Statue came from a dinner that Laboulaye had organized at his home near Versailles soon after the death of the president. A good part of the conversation was reportedly about Lincoln's death, with Laboulaye praising the American people who had taken a stand against the institution of slavery. Bartholdi recalled Laboulaye declaring, "Throughout Europe, every heart beats for Lincoln."

An idealist and pacifist, Laboulaye believed that nations should forge relationships based on respect and friendship. Moved by Lincoln's death, Laboulaye suggested the idea of a commemoration for the upcoming centennial of the United States: "If a monument was ever erected in America in memory of its independence, it would seem natural to me that it be erected through a communal effort by the two nations." It would be thus, said Laboulaye, that "we declare, through an enduring memory, the friendship that the blood shed by our fathers once sealed between the two nations."

Inspired by Bartholdi's proposal and assured that Americans would welcome the gesture, Laboulaye formed the Franco-American Union in 1875 to promote and fund this vast undertaking. In the spirit of cooperation between the countries, it was decided that the French would be responsible for raising funds for the Statue's construction and shipment via subscriptions from its citizens, while the Americans would raise funds for a pedestal to mount the Statue on Bedloe's Island. Laboulaye dubbed Bartholdi's proposed work *Liberty Enlightening the World*—it would be a monument to the friendship between two nations and a potent signal of social progress.

The "Ninth Wonder" of the World

In 1886, New York was not yet a city of skyscrapers. Few at the time imagined that the Flatiron would rise to 285 feet in 1902, the Empire State Building to 1,250 feet in 1931, and One Trade Center to 1,776 feet in 2014. The first American skyscraper was actually in Chicago— the 180-foot-high Home Insurance Building, erected in 1885. But the Statue of Liberty would rise far above it. The Statue itself measures 150 feet, from the base to the top of the torch; add on the 154-foot pedestal, and the Statue soars 304 feet above the waters of the Upper Bay. To the nineteenth-century observer, the extraordinary height of Bartholdi's monument was an overwhelming sight. The height also shows a certain hubris that even Bartholdi acknowledged in his letters to his mother, when he wrote about making his mark in history. But that wasn't the only reason why he designed his creation to be the tallest statue of its time.

Bartholdi recognized that a monument needed to be of colossal proportions to be visible in the middle of New York's immense harbor. Central to his vision was the concept of a lighthouse. In Bartholdi's mind, his lighthouse would not only symbolically illuminate the world but be of practical use as well. He would need to utilize the technological innovations of the mid-nineteenth century that enabled these immense structures to be built in the service of maritime traffic and international trade.

And the height also served to exhibit the excellence of French engineering, still vital despite France's military defeat at the hands of Prussia in 1870. The Statue of Liberty was the result of an unprecedented collaboration, that of an artist with a world-renowned engineer: Alexandre-Gustave Eiffel. A specialist in metal suspension bridges, he took over the responsibility of designing the structure that would support the Statue after the sudden death of renowned architect Eugène Viollet-le-Duc in 1879.

previous page
Construction of the Flatiron Building, 1902.

below
Portrait of Gustave Eiffel.

opposite
View from below the Eiffel Tower, Paris.

"Can one think that because we are engineers, beauty does not preoccupy us or that we do not try to build beautiful, as well as solid and long lasting structures?"

— Alexandre-Gustave Eiffel

Gustave Eiffel is best known for his Eiffel Tower, erected in 1889, which was similarly ambitious. The huge scale of Bartholdi's Statue and Eiffel's Tower conveys the sense that political progress is not divorced from material progress, that the boldness of democracy responds to a work's audacity, and that the achievements of a Republic are irreversible. At the time, the very idea of colossal statuary was progressive; it was meant as a democratic art, accessible to everyone, public, and free. As such it was the very opposite of bourgeois art, which was considered commercial, confined to private spaces, and small scale. And the time was right for Bartholdi's creation; in the United States, as in France, cities developed rapidly following the Industrial Revolution, and new spaces of urban conviviality were created, such as public parks filled with sculptures and fountains. The Statue of Liberty joined this movement.

But Bartholdi's passion for monumentalism had its origin far from France, in Egypt. The poet Baudelaire once wrote how the universe was equal to the "vast appetite" of "the child, in love with maps and prints." This description brings to mind the young Bartholdi, who was able to nourish himself with the numerous volumes in his family's library that spoke of past worlds and worlds apart. Bartholdi would be the first member of his family to leave old Europe. At a time when an interest in "the Orient" pervaded European literature and painting, he sought to explore the cradle of civilization, to "do the tour of Arabia." His artistic eye needed to be "dazzled" by "new sights."

His experiences in the East would be fundamental to his development as an artist, which he recognized near the end of his life: "I congratulate myself for having taken all the paths and traveling across a large part of the Eastern countries in my youth. If I'm at all successful, I owe it to that and still live through my former works. This is how you collect veritable treasures from which you only need to draw."

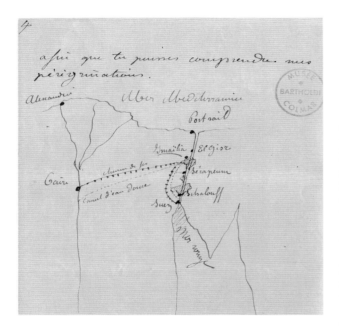

"I congratulate myself for having taken all the paths and traveling across a large part of the Eastern countries in my youth. If I'm at all successful, I owe it to that and still live through my former works. This is how you collect veritable treasures from which you only need to draw."

— Frédéric-Auguste Bartholdi

On November 8, 1855, at only twenty-one years of age, Bartholdi sailed from Marseille to Alexandria. He left France on a mission approved by the minister of public instruction and culture, who assigned him, as well as his mentor, the painter Jean-Léon Gérôme, to the "study of Egyptian antiquities, from Nubia and Palestine as well as the photographic reproduction of the principal monuments and the most remarkable human types from these different countries."

Bartholdi fell under the spell of the legendary Egyptian city, where "everything sparkles and shines, without the sun allowing for any interruption." He confided in a friend: "I can't explain to you the strange effect that the Orient produced upon me at first sight. Alexandria was phenomenal." He dreamed of Alexandria's famous lighthouse, the third-century BC technological marvel that had been destroyed centuries before, standing once again in the city's harbor.

During his seven-month-long trip, he traveled with Gérôme on the Nile, and at one point Bartholdi ventured alone, by foot and on camelback, through Abyssinia and across the Red Sea to the shores of Yemen. This region was called the "joyful Arabia"; it was the "Kingdom of Sanaa," the setting for the myth of the Queen of Sheba. Sketching as he traveled, the young sculptor filled notebooks with his drawings, capturing scenes of everyday life. This luminous land enchanted him and he would go on to make remarkable paintings of it throughout his life. Part of his mission was to utilize the then-new medium of photography, specifically the salt print, or calotype, to record scenes of antiquity. The first calotypes of Yemen are by Bartholdi; the documentation that he put together is a treasure.

top, left
Bartholdi's vision for the Suez lighthouse that he presented to the kedhive in 1869.

top, right
Sketch from Bartholdi's journal, Egypt, 1855.

bottom, left
Bartholdi took inspiration from Egyptian pyramids.

bottom, right.
Frédéric-Auguste Bartholdi, *Café on the Banks of the Nile*, 1860.

A. BARTHOLDI 1873

The young artist was fascinated by the monumentality of ancient ruins and their almost theatrical staging in dreamlike landscapes. His photographs testify to his admiration of the Karnak religious complex's grandiose remnants and how impressed he was by these raised stones, their impact undiminished after millennia. Egyptian statuary is more than an artistic manifestation; it is a challenge to the passage of time, to history, to nature, and to man. In Egypt, Bartholdi had the revelation that the mastery of such art at this scale engages the landscape, bringing sculpture closer to architecture. Perhaps the initial concept of the Statue of Liberty was born when he viewed these vestiges of the pharaohs, from Giza to Aswan, from Kom Ombo to Luxor.

His passion for Egypt—and the grandiose—stayed with him. Thirteen years later, in the spring of 1869, Bartholdi returned to Cairo for a trip of several weeks' duration. He had only one goal. Diplomat and canal builder Ferdinand de Lesseps was in the midst of completing the Suez Canal—the waterway connecting Europe to the Indian Ocean that would launch globalization—and Bartholdi wanted to convince the reigning khedive of Egypt and de Lesseps to erect an immense lighthouse at the canal's entrance.

Unfortunately for Bartholdi, both the French builder and the khedive declined to support his proposal. He brought back to France his models and sketches, and he was never to build his Egyptian lighthouse. Interestingly, de Lesseps would end up supporting another Bartholdi endeavor, when de Lesseps became the head of the Franco-American Union after Édouard de Laboulaye's death in 1883.

Models showing the evolution of Bartholdi's monument, from the Suez Canal project to the final Statue of Liberty.

Throughout his life, Bartholdi would deny that he had revisited the design of his Suez Canal project to create the Statue of Liberty; indeed, while their appearance and structure appear similar, their context and meaning are worlds apart. Regardless, a terra-cotta figurine of the Suez Canal statue in Bartholdi's studio, marked with his initials and the year, "AB 1867"—the date of the second Paris Exposition Universelle—shows a figure of an Egyptian peasant woman holding a lantern above her head. Except for the hairstyle, the model clearly presages Lady Liberty.

Six terra-cotta figurines still in existence as well as Bartholdi's sketches and watercolors show the evolution of his Suez Canal lighthouse to the Statue of Liberty, from 1867 to 1872, from Egypt to America.

In creating his own modern wonder, Bartholdi dreamed of resurrecting Alexandria's lighthouse, one of the "seven wonders" of the world. He would say to his friends that while the eighth wonder of the world was the Suez Canal, the ninth wonder of the world would be the Statue of Liberty.

The Rivet That Reaches the Sky

The Statue of Liberty took form with unprecedented speed, despite financial and practical setbacks. Soon after the Franco-American Union's formation in 1875, Bartholdi was able to refine his concept in a series of ever-more precise models and begin the daunting process of designing its support and construction. The complex process of the making of this giant incorporated age-old techniques and nineteenth-century state-of-the-art engineering, from the gigantic structure to the smallest rivet.

The Statue's skin is composed of copper plates formed by an ancient metalwork process, repoussé, in which workers hammered the sheets of copper against wooden molds to shape their contours. These plates are affixed to an armature—sturdy metal columns with a connecting trellis of smaller iron bars. Holding the copper plates together are many rivets, nineteen inches long and spaced nearly one inch apart. These special metal pins, each with a flat head like a nail, join the sheets together. During the final assembly of the Statue on Bedloe's Island, each rivet was heated and inserted in a hole that had been drilled through the copper plates. On the other side of the copper sheet, a worker then hammered the headless end of the rivet, flattening the remaining shaft to form a second head and plug the hole. Thus the assemblage's stability was guaranteed. This technique was followed over every inch of the Statue.

The riveting system was perfected by a friend of Bartholdi's, the coppersmith Antoine Durenne, who worked with him in 1886 on a fountain named after the sculptor that stands in the United States Botanic Garden in Washington, D.C. Rivets had been forged by hand, a time-consuming process, until Durenne invented a machine to manufacture rivets efficiently. It's due to this man—and the rivet—that Lady Liberty was able to reach so high.

"We only hear hammering, grinding noises of filing, clinking chains; everywhere agitation, a brouhaha, an enormous commotion. You'd think we were in a huge factory."

— A visitor to the Gaget, Gauthier & Compagnie workshops

In fact, the rivet's starring role in the Statue's assembly was recognized on October 24, 1881. In celebration of the anniversary of the British surrender at Yorktown, Virginia, the U.S. ambassador to France, Levi P. Morton, was invited to visit the Gaget, Gauthier & Compagnie workshops in Paris, where Bartholdi had arranged for the Statue to be constructed. There Morton nailed the first rivet into the first copper sheet, initiating the construction.

Beneath the Statue's skin is an ingenious metal armature—but that was not the original plan. To design the internal structure, Bartholdi first hired Eugène Viollet-le-Duc, an architect who had achieved renown through his celebrated restoration of the cathedral of Notre Dame. Typically, monuments were supported by substantial masonry that would conform to the external shell, but this arrangement would not be able to support such a large-scale work. Viollet-le-Duc had the idea of using repousséd copper sheets, which would allow the Statue's surface to retain flexibility.

To stabilize the massive work, he conceived of a system of internal sheet metal partitions that would replace masonry; these partitions would form pockets to be filled with sand. This had an added advantage: if the Statue were to be damaged, an individual interior section could be opened, the sand let out, and the damage fixed. It's because of Viollet-le-Duc that the Statue has numerous folds in its dress; their principal function was to increase the drapery's rigidity. But ultimately the Statue's innovative internal structure is due to engineer Gustave Eiffel, whom Bartholdi hired after Viollet-le-Duc's death in 1879. Eiffel would be the one to incarnate this new "iron age."

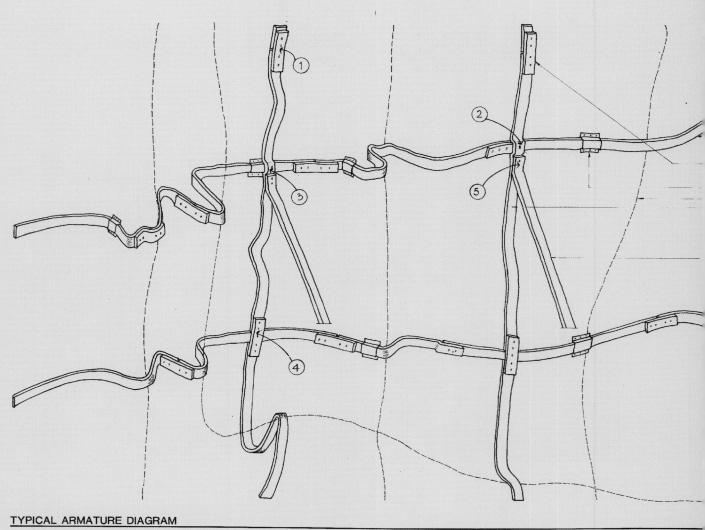

TYPICAL ARMATURE DIAGRAM

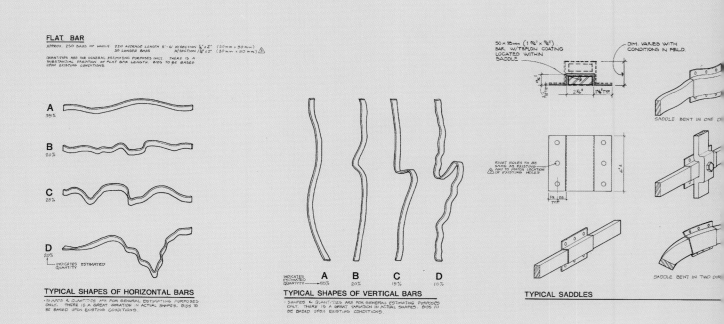

FLAT BAR

APPROX. 250 BARS OF WHICH 220 AVERAGE LENGTH 5'-6' W/SECTION ⅝"×2" (20mm × 50mm)
30 LONGER BARS W/SECTION 1¼"×2" (30mm × 50mm)

QUANTITIES ARE FOR GENERAL ESTIMATING PURPOSES ONLY. THERE IS A
SUBSTANTIAL VARIATION OF FLAT BAR LENGTH. BIDS TO BE BASED
UPON EXISTING CONDITIONS.

A 35%

B 20%

C 25%

D 20%

INDICATES ESTIMATED
QUANTITY

TYPICAL SHAPES OF HORIZONTAL BARS

· SHAPES & QUANTITIES ARE FOR GENERAL ESTIMATING PURPOSES
ONLY. THERE IS A GREAT VARIATION IN ACTUAL SHAPES. BIDS TO
BE BASED UPON EXISTING CONDITIONS.

INDICATES
ESTIMATED
QUANTITY → 55%
A **B** 20% **C** 15% **D** 10%

TYPICAL SHAPES OF VERTICAL BARS

· SHAPES & QUANTITIES ARE FOR GENERAL ESTIMATING PURPOSES
ONLY. THERE IS A GREAT VARIATION IN ACTUAL SHAPES. BIDS TO
BE BASED UPON EXISTING CONDITIONS.

50 × 15mm (1 ⁹⁄₁₆" × ⁹⁄₁₆")
BAR W/TEFLON COATING
LOCATED WITHIN
SADDLE

DIM. VARIES WITH
CONDITIONS IN FIELD

RIVET HOLES TO BE
SAME AS EXISTING
AND TO MATCH LOCATION
OF EXISTING HOLES

SADDLE BENT IN ONE D

SADDLE BENT IN TWO DIR

TYPICAL SADDLES

TYPICAL ARMATURE

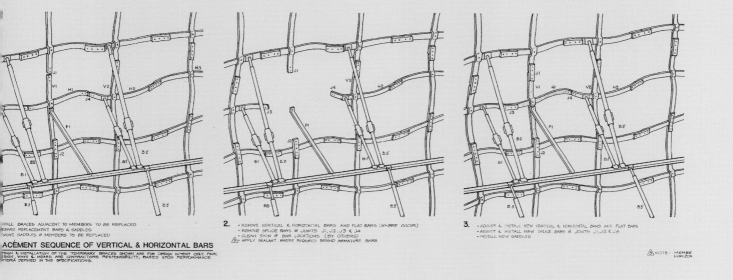

ACÉMENT SEQUENCE OF VERTICAL & HORIZONTAL BARS

STALL BRACES ADJACENT TO MEMBERS TO BE REPLACED
EPARE REPLACEMENT BARS & SADDLES
MOVE SADDLES & MEMBERS TO BE REPLACED

SIGN & INSTALLATION OF THE TEMPORARY BRACES SHOWN ARE FOR DESIGN INTENT ONLY. FINAL
SIGN, WAYS & MEANS ARE CONTRACTORS RESPONSIBILITY, BASED UPON PERFORMANCE
TERIA DEFINED IN THE SPECIFICATIONS.

2. • REMOVE VERTICAL & HORIZONTAL BARS AND FLAT BARS (WHERE OCCUR)
• REMOVE SPLICE BARS @ JOINTS J1, J2, J3 & J4
• CLEAN SKIN @ BAR LOCATIONS (BY OTHERS)
• APPLY SEALANT WHERE REQUIRED BEHIND ARMATURE BARS

3. • ADJUST & INSTALL NEW VERTICAL & HORIZONTAL BARS AND FLAT BARS
• ADJUST & INSTALL NEW SPLICE BARS @ JOINTS J1, J2 & J3
• INSTALL NEW SADDLES

NOTE: MEMBE
HORIZON

previous spread
Armature plans from the 1986 centennial restoration.

opposite
Onlookers from the Brooklyn Bridge admire the beauty of the Statue of Liberty at dusk.

below
A prototype of the Statue.

"Here, Bartholdi and his statuary assistants put the last touches on the work: one on the first level of the scaffolding fixes the mouth's crease; another, on the second level, retouches one of the eyes; the third, at the top, works on a detail of the crown which encircles this gigantic figure."

— A visitor to the rue de Chazelles pre-assembly site

Bartholdi and Eiffel were both Freemasons, and they shared a faith in progress. Eiffel, and his principal partner, the Alsatian Maurice Koechlin, decided to replace the Viollet-le-Duc system of partitions with something Eiffel knew well: a metal skeleton. Viollet-le-Duc's concept was that the copper casing would support itself, the weight of the Statue holding it in place. In the Eiffel-Koechlin plan, the casing would be suspended from and supported by an iron frame—a revolutionary shift from gravity to a kind of levity, from the oak to the reed, and the same principle on which the architecture of the modern skyscraper would be based. By flat iron armature bars fixed to the Statue's interior surface, the copper surface is connected to a large column that has four attachment points with tie rods that descend into the concrete foundation.

Once the structure holding the Statue was designed, the construction commenced, with a team of carpenters, plaster mixers, blacksmiths, and coppersmiths filling the vast Gaget, Gauthier & Compagnie workshops near Parc Monceau with sawdust and the sounds of ringing hammers. After a final clay model, Bartholdi cast a study model in plaster at one-sixteenth the size of the planned giant Statue.

Workers enlarged this again, creating another plaster model. At fully one-fourth of the size of the planned Statue, it was still small enough that the eye could easily view its totality.

Lines were traced on this model, dividing it into sections, and each section was numbered.

below and opposite
Workers and craftsmen fabricating sections of the
Statue in the Paris workshops, 1884.

p. 69
Bartholdi's technical sketches and panel of
specifications for the Statue.

pp. 71–72
Bartholdi within the Statue's left hand assembly in
the Paris workshops, 1884.

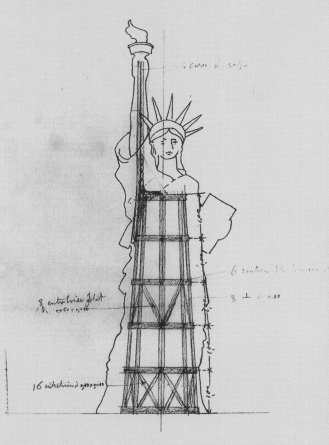

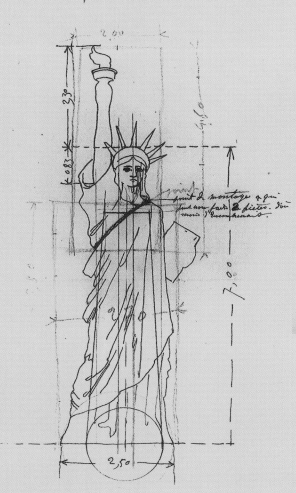

DIMENSIONS

OF THE

☙ STATUE OF LIBERTY ☙

Presented by France and Erected in 1886
On Bedloe's Island, New York Harbor.

	Ft.	in.
Height from base to torch	151	1
Foundation of pedestal to torch	305	6
Heel to top of hand	111	6
Length of hand	16	5
Index Finger	8	0
Circumference at second joint	7	6
Size of finger nail	13x10	
Head from chin to cranium	17	3
Head, thickness from ear to ear	10	0
Distance across the eye	2	6
Length of nose	4	6
Right arm, length	42	0
Right arm, greatest thickness	12	0
Thickness of waist	35	0
Width of mouth	3	0
Tablet, length	23	7
" width	13	7
" thickness	2	0

DIMENSIONS OF PEDESTAL.

	Ft.	in.
Height of pedestal	89	0
Square sides at base, each	62	0
" " " top, "	40	0
Grecian Columns, above base	72	8

DIMENSIONS OF FOUNDATION.

	Ft.	in.
Height of foundation	65	0
Square sides at bottom	91	0
" " " top	66	7

The statue weighs 450,000 pounds or 225 tons. The bronze alone weighs 200,000 pounds. Forty persons can stand comfortably in the head, and the torch will hold 12 people.

The number of steps in the statue from the pedestal to the head, is 154, and the ladder leading up through the extended right arm to the torch has 54 rounds.

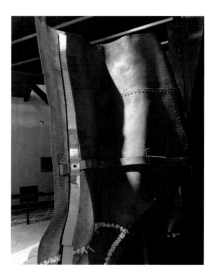

"[The Statue's] part is not to appear extraordinary in itself, but to connect itself intimately with an extraordinary whole."

— Frédédéric-Auguste Bartholdi

These numbered sections were then each reproduced in larger sections four times their size. These, in turn, were assembled on a lattice-work frame, which was then covered in plaster. The measurements were checked once more, and these pieces were used to create full-size wooden molds to shape the copper skin of the Statue.

Using the repoussé method, the workers pounded copper sheets that were 3/32nd of an inch thick with mallets until the sheets matched the contours of the wooden molds. Workers assembled three hundred of these pieces, each more than three square feet to more than nine square feet in area and all totaling 176,369 pounds, on the iron framework. The provisional assembly in France was done with screws. The final assembly, on the Bedloe's Island site in the United States, would be more elaborate, entailing three hundred thousand copper rivets, their flattened heads nearly invisible on the exterior surface. The assembled sections would give the impression of having been constructed from one solid piece.

While still under construction in Paris, the Statue received many visitors. All one needed was an admission card to visit on Mondays and Thursdays, from noon to five o'clock. The racket was deafening, wrote one visitor: "We only hear hammering, grinding noises of filing, clinking chains; everywhere agitation, a brouhaha, an enormous commotion. You'd think we were in a huge factory." The most impressive visitor to the Statue was the famed poet and novelist Victor Hugo, who was accompanied by his granddaughter. For a long time, Hugo silently stood before Lady Liberty and then said: "The ocean, this grand, restless thing, observes the union of two large pacified lands." Bartholdi presented him with a gift, a piece of copper from the construction on which had been inscribed: "To Victor Hugo / The workers of the Franco-American Union. / Piece of the colossal statue of liberty presented to the illustrious apostle of Peace, Liberty, and Progress. / Victor Hugo / The day that he honored the work of the Franco-American Union with his visit."

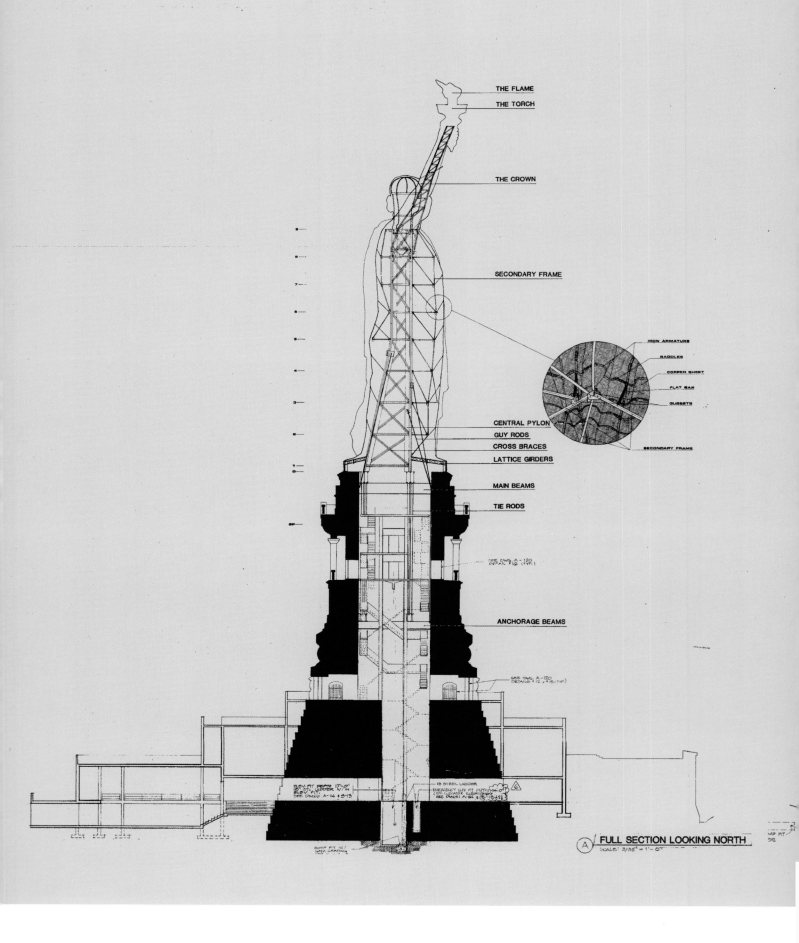

THE FLAME

THE TORCH

THE CROWN

SECONDARY FRAME

IRON ARMATURE

SADDLES

COPPER SHEET

FLAT BAR

GUSSETS

SECONDARY FRAME

CENTRAL PYLON

GUY RODS

CROSS BRACES

LATTICE GIRDERS

MAIN BEAMS

TIE RODS

SEE DWG. A-120
DETAIL #12 (TYP.)

ANCHORAGE BEAMS

SEE DWG. A-120
DETAILS #12 & #15 (TYP.)

ELEV. PIT DEPTH 17'-0"
(18 STL. LADDER W/IN
ELEV. PIT).
SEE DWGS. A-114 & B-13

1B STEEL LADDER

EMERGENCY ELEV. PIT DEPTH 15'-0"
(STP. ELEVATOR ELEVATION)
SEE DWGS. A-116 & B-13A

SUMP PIT W/
GALV. GRATING

Ⓐ **FULL SECTION LOOKING NORTH**
SCALE: 3/32" = 1'-0"

MP PIT
542

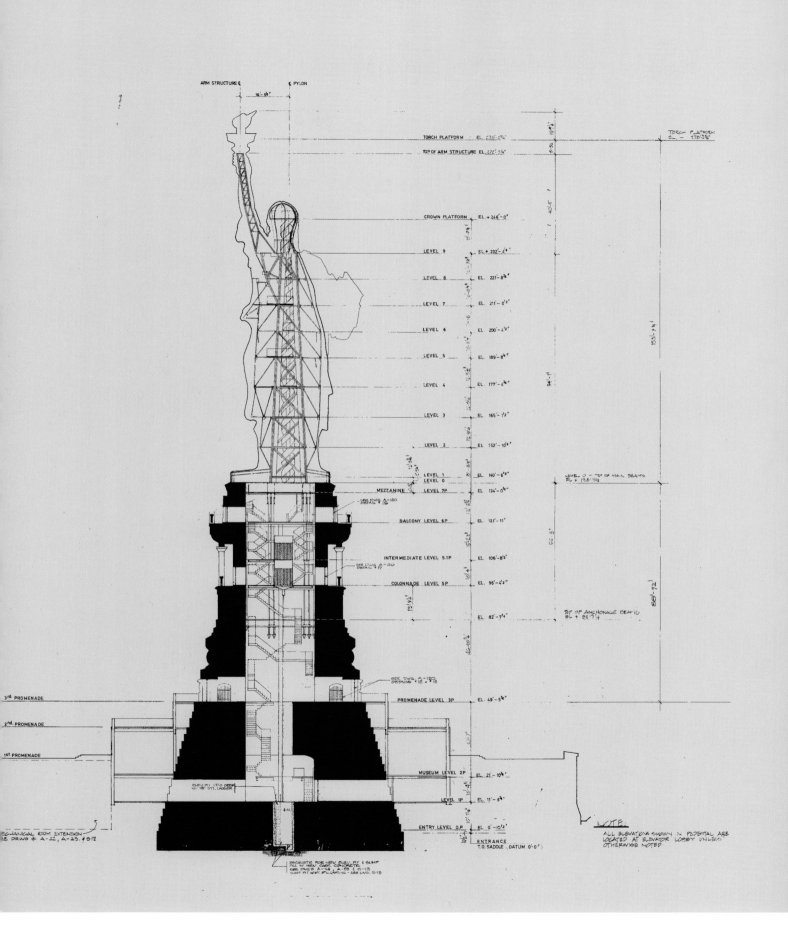

In May 1884, *Scientific American* published a magnificent engraving of the Statue, which had been assembled, piece by piece, like an immense jigsaw puzzle on the rue de Chazelles in Paris, not far from the Parc Monceau. This preliminary assembly of the Statue not only tested the engineering before the long voyage to the United States, but also served to promote the Statue, which fascinated French and foreign journalists: "It's one of the most curious spectacles that can be imagined, and we witnessed it yesterday for more than two hours without getting tired of it.

"Here, Bartholdi and his statuary assistants put the last touches on the work: one on the first level of the scaffolding fixes the mouth's crease; another, on the second level, retouches one of the eyes; the third, at the top, works on a detail of the crown which encircles this gigantic figure." Artists such as Victor Dargaud and Luigi Loir showed the Statue wedged between two brand-new Hausmannian buildings of which one, blue in color, displays an advertisement for *Le Petit Journal*. Corseted in wooden scaffolding and its size overwhelming the neighborhood, the Statue was drawn and photographed, its image etched and engraved and disseminated in periodicals around the globe.

In the United States, the design of a suitable pedestal for the Statue was in the hands of Richard Morris Hunt. He and Bartholdi sent sketches to each other, rejecting a tall tower and a structure based on a Mesoamerican pyramid before agreeing on a neoclassical design that would enhance the Statue without overshadowing it. Hunt incorporated the walls of the star-shaped Fort Wood on Bedloe's Island, and army engineer General Charles P. Stone designed a twenty-seven-thousand-ton concrete core that extended below the foundation of the pedestal to anchor the Statue.

However, the American members of the Franco-American Union were finding that raising funds for the construction of the pedestal was alarmingly difficult—many Americans didn't seem to understand the Statue's relevance. Hunt donated his usual fee to help with fundraising efforts, but without financial support, the construction of the pedestal lagged, even as the Statue took shape in Paris.

Finally, Bartholdi's creation was dismantled for the long trip across the Atlantic. In an immense hangar, more than two hundred wooden crates measuring thirteen feet long and more than eight feet wide held the Statue's 350 pieces, the heaviest parcel weighing around 1,763 pounds.

In total there were 264,554 pounds of iron and 176,369 pounds of copper. Rivets, washers, and nuts and bolts alone took up thirty-six crates. Gigantic cranes were installed at the Saint-Lazare train station, where the cargo was loaded into the hold of the French frigate *Isère*. Then at long last, on May 21, 1885, the ship departed Rouen to bring France's gift to its American abode.

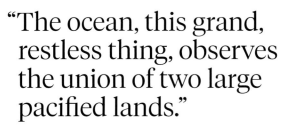

"The ocean, this grand, restless thing, observes the union of two large pacified lands."

— Victor Hugo

The Light of the Torch

The torch that the Statue of Liberty holds aloft—a beacon of enlightenment, shining brightly by day and glowing at night—is what immediately distinguishes the Statue within New York Harbor.

In this meeting place of megapolis and ocean, Bartholdi knew that a prominent gesture was needed, simple enough to be read at a distance yet at such a scale that its impact would not dissipate within the vast landscape. Otherwise, as Bartholdi said, "She would be halfway devoured by the surrounding space's immensity; she would drown in the illuminated or foggy layers of air." The art of the colossal, as Eugène Lesbazeilles wrote in *Les Colosses anciens et modernes* (Ancient and Modern Colossi) (1881), must affirm "the type of effect that a large tree has on us, a tall mountain, the ocean, the roaring of wind, rolling thunder." Functioning in much the same way and also meant to be seen from afar, the lighthouse as a concept had already appeared in Bartholdi's proposed Egyptian monument for the Suez Canal. One of his early concepts for the Statue of Liberty showed the lighting emanating from the crown and not the torch, which would have primarily an aesthetic function, creating a dynamic sense of movement. But he also meant the torch to be symbolic, the meaning of which is integral to the creator's intent.

"Instead of holding lightning bolts that carry terror and death in her hand, she supports the torch that guides men toward the path of freedom."

— President Grover Cleveland, dedication of the Statue of Liberty, 1886

Bartholdi wanted his monument to "light up the world."
The light would lift the world out of darkness through
reason, education, and free will, empowering people
to engage and participate in democracy. The light of
knowledge and the flame of individual conscience would
knock down false beliefs, foil religious and political
dogmas, and defeat tyrannies. For Bartholdi and his
liberal-thinking French and American friends, the
torch proclaimed the importance of republican values
for the world. An editorial cartoon by Alfred Le Petit,
published in *La Revue tintamarresque* during Paris's
1878 Exposition Universelle, tellingly portrays the Statue
of Liberty sweeping away with her immense thumb the
monarchist thrones and crowns from the planet.

"The large arm is erected
and I would say without
any modesty, it's a
beautiful piece and very
striking."

— Frédéric-Auguste Bartholdi

This meaning also appears on the tablet held in the Statue's left hand, on which is the inscription "July, 4, 1776." This is the date of the Declaration of Independence of the United States, and the tablet signifies the book of law: in a democracy, law should reign over the relationships between people and their rulers, because only the law will restrain arbitrariness and violence. This interpretation was shared by *The World*, the New York newspaper owned by Joseph Pulitzer that played an essential role in efforts to drum up public support for the Statue throughout the United States, especially for the construction of the pedestal.

The World helped popularize the Statue of Liberty's meaning for the American public, proclaiming on October 29, 1886—the day after the Statue's dedication— that the Statue showed that an "unlimited space for Liberty, Order, and the Law" exists "but only a parcel of land for Excessiveness, Disorder, and Anarchy." President Grover Cleveland similarly framed it during the Statue of Liberty's dedication in 1886: "Instead of holding lightning bolts that carry terror and death in her hand, she supports the torch that guides men toward the path of freedom." The torch is the flame that illuminates to see better and farther, not a fire that sets ablaze or destroys.

Another reference to the political issue of emancipation lies beneath Lady Liberty's left foot: a broken chain. This symbol cannot be more subtle, practically concealed from view whether seen from afar or close to the Statue. An allegorical painting by Bartholdi's teacher Ary Scheffer inspired him to include the chain: *Christ rémunérateur* (*Christus Remunerator*) (1847), a reproduction of which Bartholdi's mother, Charlotte, had bought in 1853. In the painting one distinguishes the tyrant and the slave behind whom there are not only— according to Scheffer himself in a letter to a cousin—"the revolt with the torch and dagger," but also a broken chain.

BY AUTHORITY OF THE AMERICAN COMMITTEE OF THE STATUE OF LIBERTY.

Another painting of Scheffer's, *Christ consolateur* (*Christus Consolatur*) (1851), also denounced the injustices of his time, portraying a dead child, a suicide, a shipwrecked sailor, an exile, a Polish person fighting against the Russians, a Greek man resisting the Turks, and a chained black man. Scheffer and Bartholdi and others of their liberal circles were abolitionists and cherished the ideals of an American republic. For Bartholdi, the broken chain under the Statue's feet not only depicted the end of slavery (and alluded to Lincoln and his assassination), but also addressed men of liberty, encouraging them to break the chains of oppression while avoiding a violent revolution.

Chauncey M. Depew, one of Bartholdi's greatest supporters, also a Freemason and president of the Union League, brought a further issue to the forefront in his speech at the unveiling of the Statue in 1886: "The problems of capital and labor, of social regeneration and moral growth, of property and poverty, resolve themselves under the beneficial influence of an illuminated liberty, capable of founding and respecting its laws; there won't be a need for the help of kings or armies, neither that of anarchists or bombs." He was referring to a wave of anti-capitalist sentiment within the United States at that time. Earlier, in 1881, Henry George, who would be an unsuccessful candidate to the office of New York mayor in 1886, had denounced in *Progress and Poverty* the contradictions of capitalism and the illusion of liberty without social or economic freedom. However, in holding up the French Revolution as an ideal, he becomes the "red phantom"—an instigator of bloody rebellion—and he clearly references the Statue when he declares: "We lit a torch of which they will not be able to extinguish the flame."

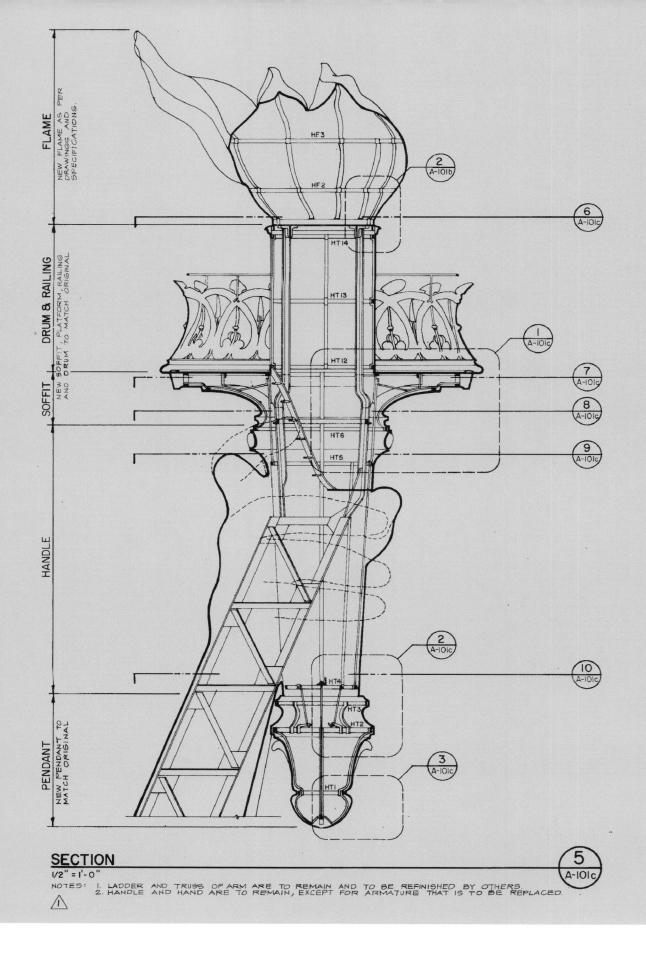

FLAME

NEW FLAME AS PER DRAWINGS AND SPECIFICATIONS.

HF3

HF2

DRUM & RAILING

NEW SOFFIT, PLATFORM, RAILING AND DRUM TO MATCH ORIGINAL

HT14

HT13

HT12

SOFFIT

HT6

HT5

HANDLE

HT4

PENDANT

NEW PENDANT TO MATCH ORIGINAL

HT3

HT2

HT1

SECTION

1/2" = 1'-0"

NOTES: 1. LADDER AND TRUSS OF ARM ARE TO REMAIN AND TO BE REFINISHED BY OTHERS.
2. HANDLE AND HAND ARE TO REMAIN, EXCEPT FOR ARMATURE THAT IS TO BE REPLACED.

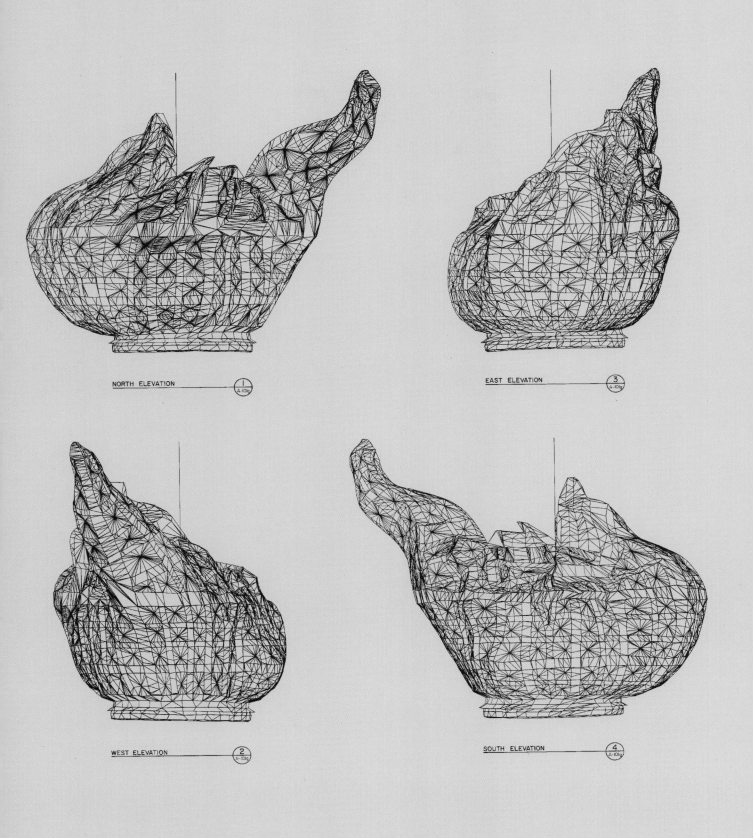

NORTH ELEVATION ①
A-101g

EAST ELEVATION ③
A-101g

WEST ELEVATION ②
A-101g

SOUTH ELEVATION ④
A-101g

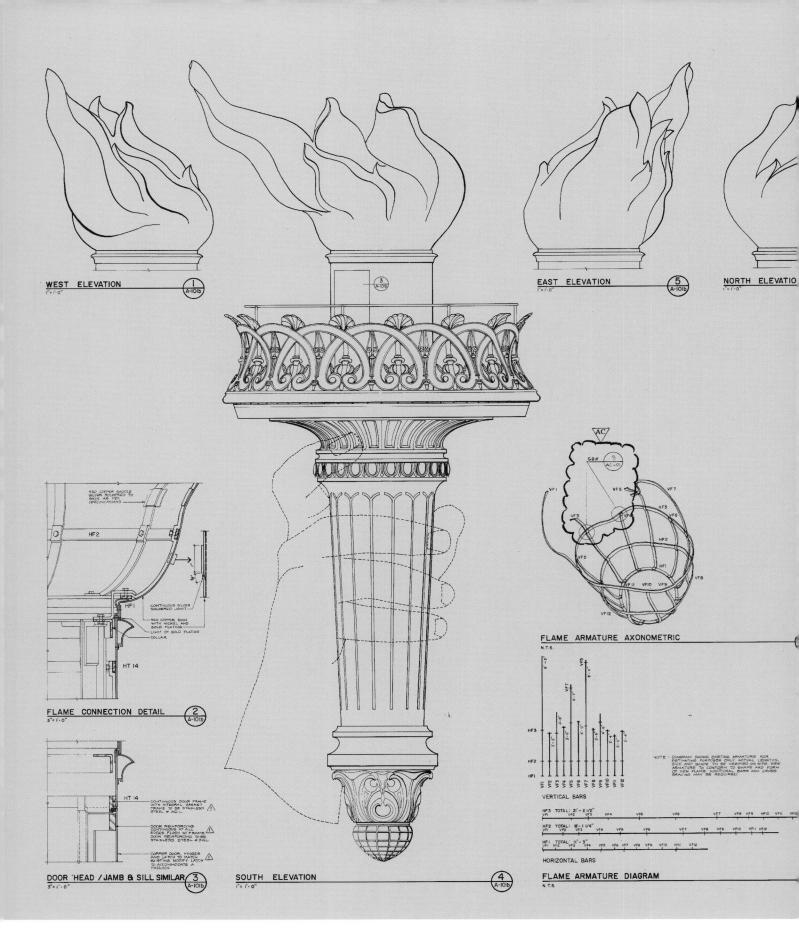

WEST ELEVATION ①
1"=1'-0" A-101b

EAST ELEVATION ⑤
1"=1'-0" A-101b

NORTH ELEVATIO
1"=1'-0"

FLAME CONNECTION DETAIL ②
3"=1'-0" A-101b

DOOR HEAD / JAMB & SILL SIMILAR ③
3"=1'-0" A-101b

SOUTH ELEVATION ④
1"=1'-0" A-101b

FLAME ARMATURE AXONOMETRIC
N.T.S.

FLAME ARMATURE DIAGRAM
N.T.S.

VERTICAL BARS

HORIZONTAL BARS

NOTE: DIAGRAM SHOWS EXISTING ARMATURE FOR
ESTIMATING PURPOSES ONLY. ACTUAL LENGTHS,
SIZES AND SHAPE TO BE VERIFIED ON SITE. NEW
ARMATURE TO CONFORM TO SHAPE AND FORM
OF NEW FLAME. ADDITIONAL BARS AND CROSS
BRACING MAY BE REQUIRED.

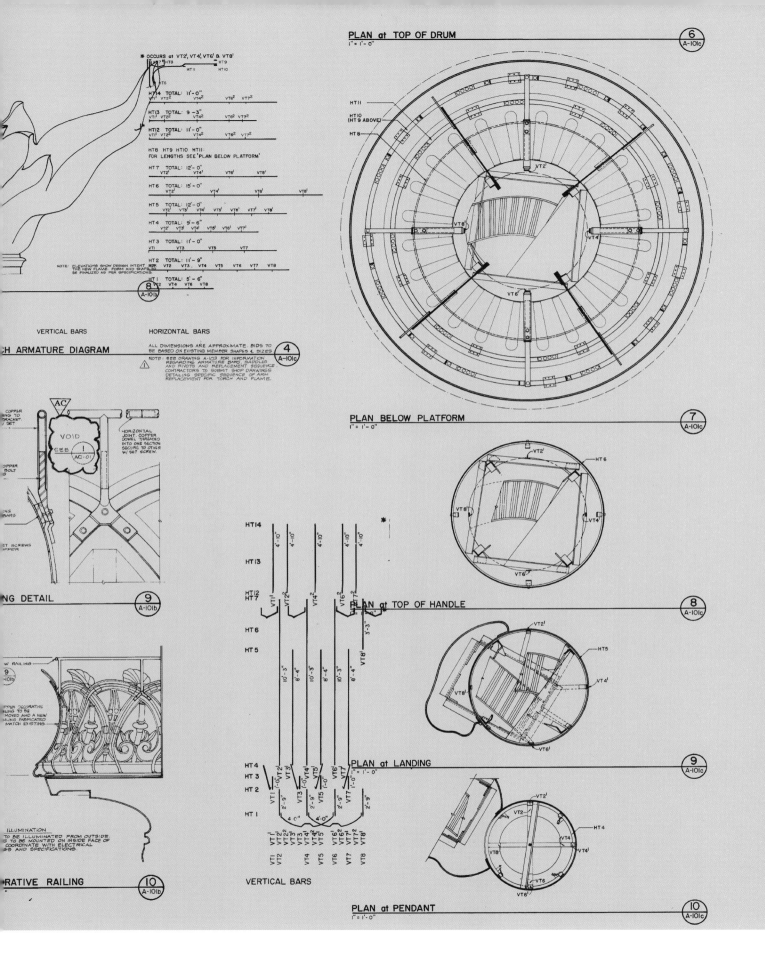

* OCCURS at VT2¹, VT4¹, VT6¹ & VT8¹

HT14 TOTAL: 11'-0"
HT13 TOTAL: 9'-3"
HT12 TOTAL: 11'-0"

HT8 HT9 HT10 HT11
FOR LENGTHS SEE 'PLAN BELOW PLATFORM'

HT7 TOTAL: 12'-0"
HT6 TOTAL: 15'-0"
HT5 TOTAL: 12'-0"
HT4 TOTAL: 9'-6"
HT3 TOTAL: 11'-0"
HT2 TOTAL: 11'-9"

NOTE: ELEVATIONS SHOW DESIGN INTENT FOR THE NEW FLAME. FORM AND SHAPE TO BE FINALIZED AS PER SPECIFICATIONS.

HT1 TOTAL: 5'-6"
8
A-101b

VERTICAL BARS   HORIZONTAL BARS

CH ARMATURE DIAGRAM

ALL DIMENSIONS ARE APPROXIMATE. BIDS TO BE BASED ON EXISTING MEMBER SHAPES & SIZES.

NOTE: SEE DRAWING A-103 FOR INFORMATION REGARDING ARMATURE BARS, SADDLES AND RIVETS AND REPLACEMENT SEQUENCE. CONTRACTORS TO SUBMIT SHOP DRAWINGS DETAILING SPECIFIC SEQUENCE OF ARM REPLACEMENT FOR TORCH AND FLAME.

4
A-101c

AC

COPPER RING TO BRACKET SET

VOID SEE 1 AC-01

HORIZONTAL JOINT. COPPER DOWEL THREADED INTO ONE SECTION SECURE TO OTHER W/ SET SCREW.

COPPER BOLT

SET SCREWS COPPER

NG DETAIL
9
A-101b

9
A-101b

W RAILING

COPPER DECORATIVE RAILING TO BE MOVED AND A NEW RAILING FABRICATED MATCH EXISTING

ILLUMINATION
TO BE ILLUMINATED FROM OUTSIDE. TO BE MOUNTED ON INSIDE FACE OF COORDINATE WITH ELECTRICAL AND SPECIFICATIONS.

RATIVE RAILING
10
A-101b

PLAN BELOW PLATFORM
1" = 1'-0"
7
A-101c

PLAN at TOP OF HANDLE
8
A-101c

PLAN at LANDING
9
A-101c

PLAN at PENDANT
1" = 1'-0"
10
A-101c

HT14
HT13
HT12
HT7
HT6
HT5

HT4
HT3
HT2
HT1

VERTICAL BARS

The torch was the first piece of the Statue to be shown
to the public through press etchings, artists' works,
and exhibitions in France and the United States.
These opportunities offered an idea of the scope of the
monument to come and, in so doing, served to publicize
the Statue. It was exhibited in Philadelphia on the
occasion of the Centennial Exposition, which opened
in May 1876. Bartholdi's second trip to the United States
was to attend this world's fair.

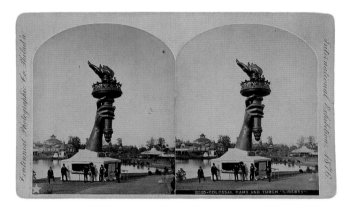

"We lit a torch of which
they will not be able to
extinguish the flame."

— Henry George

Bartholdi's idea to exhibit the hand holding the torch at
that event was ingenious. However, the assembly of the
hand took longer than anticipated, despite the assistance
of engineer Henri Stucklé. Then, as they were moving the
plaster model that was the mold for the copper sheets,
the piece broke. After lengthy delays, the hand and
torch were finally displayed in Philadelphia on October
3, 1876. Angry that by then the Fair would soon end, on
November 10, Bartholdi confided to his mother: "I went
through a lot of trouble and problems."

top, left and right
The arm and torch were on display in New York City's Madison Square between 1876 and 1882.

bottom, left
The hand and torch being assembled for display at the Philadelphia Centennial Exposition, 1876.

bottom, right
Historic rendering of visitors in the torch, 1886.

PUTTING ARM IN POSITION AT MADISON SQUARE.

THE ARM OF BARTHOLDI'S COLOSSAL STATUE OF LIBERTY.
NOW ERECTED ON A TEMPORARY PEDESTAL IN MADISON SQUARE.

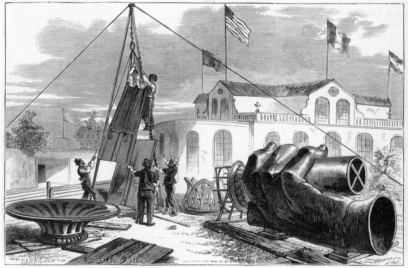

États-Unis. — Arrivée a Philadelphie des premieres parties de la statue colossale de la *Liberté*.
Fondue en France et destinée à être placée à l'entrée du port de New-York.

Nevertheless, the exhibition of the torch was an immediate success. "The large arm is erected and I would say without any modesty," Bartholdi wrote to Charlotte, "it's a beautiful piece and very striking." To help with the fundraising efforts for the pedestal, the Frenchman adopted American-style publicity: he allowed visitors to enter the torch—for a fee.

The torch's base was transformed into a souvenir stand, where products derived from the Statue were sold: lithographs, photographs, medals, and samples of the copper sheets. Captioned "Bartholdi's Liberty - Hand and Torch," the photographs especially were a huge success. For three hundred dollars, visitors could buy one of two hundred three-foot-tall terra-cotta replicas of the Statue, labeled "Models of the Committee," signed by the creator and numbered.

Bartholdi arranged to transport the hand holding the torch to New York, where, after the Centennial Exposition, it would stand at the intersection of Broadway and Fifth Avenue, in Madison Square. But money was needed to do this.

To energize the American efforts to raise money for the pedestal and the reception of the Statue, the American Committee of the Franco-American Union was formed, under the direction of John Jay, a former ambassador who had been a friend of Laboulaye's, as well as one of the founders of the Union League; the industrialist Richard Butler; and William M. Evarts, an influential legal expert who had been close to the reform-minded Senator Charles Sumner. This committee was divided into subcommittees, each in charge of a particular mission: public subscription, private shows, publicity and printing, the site, and artistic questions.

The exhibition of the Statue of Liberty's hand and torch popularized the project, but Bartholdi lamented the small returns on the fundraising. He again confided to his mother, "I would like to stoke the subscription's momentum. The elements are all prepared, I only need the spark, which I'm waiting for." However, good news arrived on February 2, 1877: Congress officially approved the use of Bedloe's Island, where the Statue of Liberty would take its place, and made provision for its reception and permanent maintenance. It was the first victory of what felt to Bartholdi to be a long fight.

For nearly a century, the Statue held its light high, but damage from exposure to the elements took its toll on the torch. In 1984, the torch was taken down. Its replacement. an exact replica, featured a gilded flame. This torch shone brightly at the Statue of Liberty's one hundredth anniversary in 1986. The original torch is now the centerpiece of the new Statue of Liberty Museum— best viewed with the Statue of Liberty just beyond it. Bartholdi's torch has continued to serve as a beacon of shared values: in 1987, a replica of the original torch was offered to Paris by the *International Herald Tribune* for the newspaper's centennial, and installed on the Place de l'Alma.

Who Was Lady Liberty?

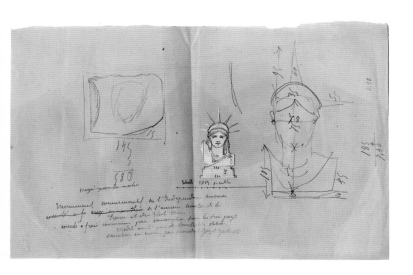

Bartholdi never explicitly identified the model for the Statue, but there are many clues throughout his work and writing as to why he chose a woman to personify Liberty.

Many have speculated that the model for the Statue's famous features was Bartholdi's wife, Jeanne-Émilie, whom he married in Newport, Rhode Island, in 1876. Others have suggested that the Statue was based on his mother or the fiancée of Bartholdi's United States lawyer, Adolphe Salmon. Still others have proposed the Duchess of Camposelice, the widow of sewing-machine inventor Isaac Singer, a woman of great beauty who welcomed artists at her Paris mansion on avenue Kléber.
The model could have been a girl at a barricade and holding a torch whom Bartholdi had glimpsed the day after the coup d'etat of Louis-Napoléon Bonaparte; a prostitute of the Pigalle district named Celine, who had once posed for him; and even the artist's brother, who suffered a mental breakdown in 1864.

If Bartholdi had wanted to pay homage to a particular woman, it stands to reason that he would have depicted her traits at the very start of his planning stages. Instead, the features portrayed in the first terra-cotta figurines dating from the 1860s for his proposed Suez Canal lighthouse—arguably the beginnings of the Statue of Liberty—were those of an idealized Egyptian peasant woman. The first preparatory sketch of the Statue of Liberty, in 1870, as well as drawings intended for the presentation of the official maquette, portray a woman whose features are universal rather than identifiable.

Bartholdi sought to capture an "idea," not an individual, in keeping with the allegorical function of the monument. The Statue's androgynous face is one that is found quite often in numerous statues of antiquity, and Bartholdi himself would use the features again, in his 1895 Basel monument recognizing Switzerland's humanitarian aid to Strasbourg during the Franco-Prussian War. In *La Suisse secourant les douleurs de Strasbourg lors du siège de 1870* (Switzerland Relieving Strasbourg's Pains During the Siege of 1870), the Helvetian figure shares similar features with *Liberty Enlightening the World*.

p. 110
A boy gets a closeup view of the Statue's face in the original Statue of Liberty Museum.

previous page
Study of the positioning of the Statue of Liberty's head on a temporary base that was exhibited during the 1878 Paris World Fair.

opposite
The Statue of Liberty's face awaits the final assembly in New York.

The idealized features of the Statue of Liberty were chosen to inspire contemplation and respect for the lofty ideals of a democratic republic. As the newspaper *Le Messager Franco-Américain* stated in 1875: "It's a sublime abstraction, which all men understand and which suffices to transform people and give birth to heroes. Does the name Liberty not electrify entire nations? Is it not heard from Europe to America?"

Could the choice of a woman been Bartholdi's acknowledgment of the nineteenth century's burgeoning feminist movement? While Bartholdi never indicated that this was the case, the Statue became an early feminist symbol. Before the unveiling of the Statue in 1886, the New York State Woman Suffrage Association asked to participate in the celebratory parade. The request was denied. The association's president, Lillie Devereux Blake, denounced this ostracism, and declared, "In erecting a Statue of Liberty embodied as a woman in a land where no woman has political liberty, men have shown a delightful inconsistency." Bartholdi certainly wouldn't have been hostile to this interpretation. His family values and philosophy inclined him to view women as equal to men. His mother, whom he admired, was an everyday example of a self-sufficient woman.

"In erecting a Statue of Liberty embodied as a woman in a land where no woman has political liberty, men have shown a delightful inconsistency."

— Lillie Devereux Blake

opposite
Visitors descend from the crown inside the Statue, 1962.

below, left
Detail of a sketch showing the positioning of the Statue's head on a temporary base that was exhibited during the 1878 Exposition Universelle.

below, right
Le Monde Illustré cover illustration showing visitors inside the Statue's head during the 1878 Exposition Universelle.

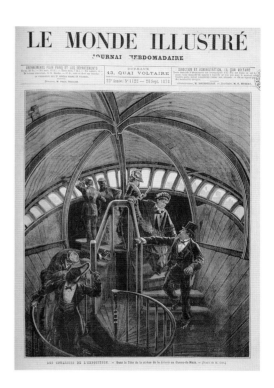

Certainly there was another woman who inspired Bartholdi: the Egyptian goddess Isis, wife of Osiris. During his trip to the Middle East in 1856, Bartholdi photographed temples that were dedicated to her. In several letters, Bartholdi discussed his "great priestess." Isis is the "revealer of mysteries" he wrote; she personifies "gnosis," the esoteric knowledge of the enlightened. The artist consecrated a work to her, a stele, called *Mystère d'Isis* (Mystery of Isis) (see page 127). Its title is hidden *in aenigmate* at the stele's base; unreadable from head-on, the title only appears when viewed at a diagonal. The scene represents an old man, carrying the phylactery of knowledge, who shares his wisdom with a beardless young man. The ceremony is presided over by a pharaoh. In the corner of the stele, Isis is breastfeeding her son, Horus.

Bartholdi was rarely represented in his works, but one example is his 1860 Colmar monument to Martin Schongauer, in which he modeled one of the smaller statues that frame the monument, a figure of a goldsmith, after himself. Those same features—Bartholdi's own—are found in the young man of *Mystère d'Isis*.

This enigmatic work was created in 1874, when Bartholdi entered into the Freemasons Lodge and he prepared the final mock-up for the Statue of Liberty. For Bartholdi, the Statue symbolized knowledge as a source of progress and liberation, and the Grand Lodge of New York laid the pedestal's cornerstone two years before the unveiling.

below, left
An illustration of the Statue of Liberty's head on display during the 1878 Exposition Universelle.

below, right
Illustration of the final assembly on Bedloe's Island.

pp. 118–119
The 1986 centennial restoration.

pp. 120–121
Technical drawings from the 1986 centennial restoration.

LA STATUE DE LA LIBERTÉ A NEW-YORK. — LA FIN DU MONTAGE

Like many artists of the nineteenth century, Bartholdi would have been familiar with French republican iconography. In France, "Marianne" is a popular and significant republican symbol, appearing in the Seal of the French Republic and as a celebrated bust by Théodore Doriot in the French Senate. But Bartholdi distanced his monument from the kind of heroic female "Marianne" figure in *Liberty Leading the People*, painted in 1830 by Eugéne Delacroix.

Peaceful and serene, the Statue of Liberty is not the French Revolution. Its stern features seem to express the liberal republicans' condemnation of political violence. Laboulaye, the project's founder, described this difference in an 1876 speech: "[Liberty] is an effort of the mind, rather than the arms"—a difference further emphasized by the illuminating torch and the tablet of law the Statue carries in its hands.

In Bartholdi's mind, just as Isis was the mother of gods, Lady Liberty would be the mother of peace.

During the 1886 unveiling of the Statue, the French consul to New York underscored just that point, that the Statue of Liberty served as a project of international accord during a time in Europe that was rife with aggressive nationalism: "It means, in brief, the extiction of bloody struggles and the union of all peoples, through the study of science, the respect of the law, and the sympathy for the weak." To Bartholdi, liberty personified as an woman embodied action as well as ideals; as the Statue takes a step forward, so people should commit to democracy liberating the world.

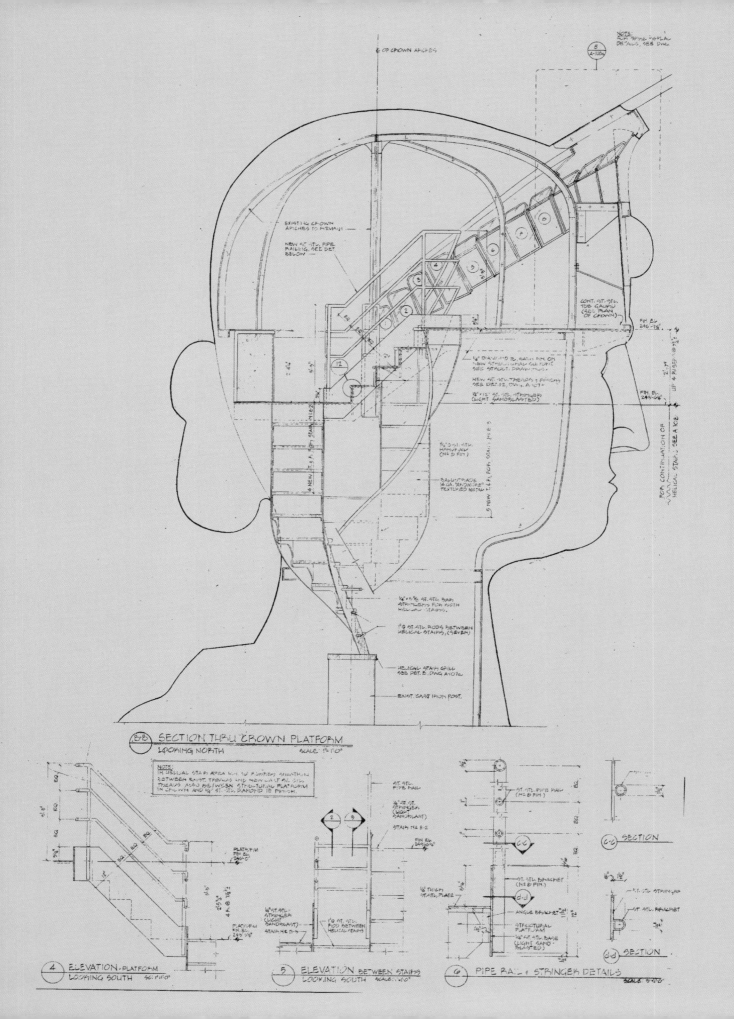

SECTION THRU CROWN PLATFORM
LOOKING NORTH   SCALE 1"=1'-0"

ELEVATION - PLATFORM
LOOKING SOUTH

ELEVATION BETWEEN STAIRS
LOOKING SOUTH   SCALE 1"=1'-0"

PIPE RAIL & STRINGER DETAILS
SCALE 3"=1'-0"

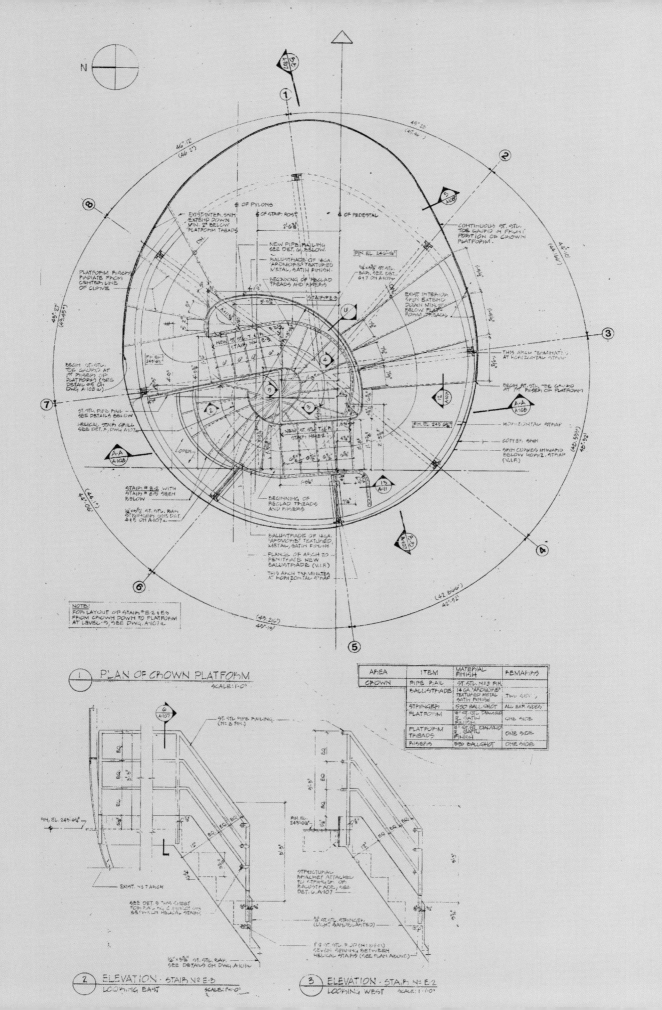

PLAN OF CROWN PLATFORM
SCALE: 1'-0"

AREA	ITEM	MATERIAL FINISH	REMARKS
CROWN	PIPE RAIL	ST. STL. N≗ 8 FIN.	
	BALUSTRADE	14 GA. "ARDMORE" TEXTURED METAL SATIN FINISH	TWO SIDES
	STRINGER	550 BALLSHOT	ALL BAR AREAS
	PLATFORM	4" ST. STL. DIAMOND PL. SATIN FINISH	ONE SIDE
	PLATFORM TREADS	4" ST. STL. DIAMOND PL. SATIN FINISH	ONE SIDE
	RISERS	550 BALLSHOT	ONE SIDE

ELEVATION · STAIR N≗ E-3
LOOKING EAST   SCALE: 1'-0"

ELEVATION · STAIR N≗ E-2
LOOKING WEST   SCALE: 1'-0"

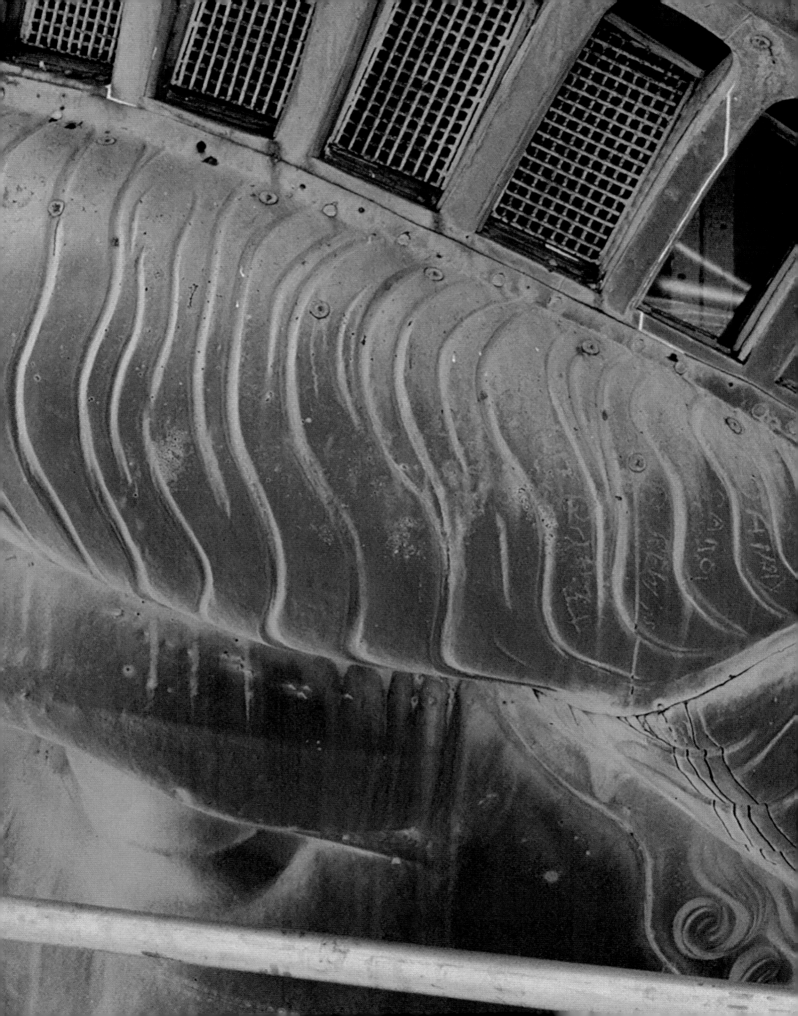

The Crown and Seven Points

Visitors to the Statue of Liberty hike up more than 375 stairs to the crown's observation windows to enjoy a unique vantage point: from three hundred feet above New York Harbor and Liberty Island, it is possible to place oneself in the mind of the artist. The head of the Statue of Liberty, its crown adorned with the rays like the sun, had its inspiration in both the past and the future.

It was not unusual for a nineteenth-century sculptor to place a many-pointed diadem symbolizing the sun upon the head of a figure. One such crown is found on a statue representing "The New Law," sculpted by Camillo Pacetti in 1810 for the facade of the cathedral of Milan, which Bartholdi is known to have visited. Another European statue dedicated to liberty has a startling resemblance to the famous New York landmark: at the Basilica of Santa Croce in Florence stands a work by sculptor Pio Fedi, commemorating Giovanni Battista Niccolini, an Italian playwright and hero of the Italian reunification movement. When it was inaugurated in 1883, Italian newspaper *La Vedetta, Gazzetta del Populo* called it "Statua della Libertà." Both statues are of Greco-Roman female figures, draped in vestal garments of antiquity. Each has its right arm raised and wears a diadem— Bartholdi's decorated with seven rays, and Fedi's with eight rays. Both New York and Florence statues include broken chains, a symbol of emancipation; Fedi's statue holds a chain in its left hand, while a chain is found under the foot of Bartholdi's monument. The statue in Florence bears no torch and wears a laurel wreath, a reference to the Greek god of poetry, Apollo.

Fedi and Bartholdi may have been inspired by the same work. On the occasion of the first French Exposition Universelle in Paris, in 1855, the immense Palais de l'Industrie was built along the Champs-Elysées. Its long facade was surmounted by a group of allegorical figures, *France Distributing Wreaths to Trade and Industry*, the work of sculptor Elias Robert. At this world's fair, too, the young Bartholdi was exhibiting his very first monument: a large statue of Alsatian hero General Count Jean Rapp. Too enormous to fit through the doors of the Palais de l'Industrie, Bartholdi's monument was permitted to be placed directly outside the venue, which served to bolster Bartholdi's reputation as a sculptor.

Elias Robert's statue clearly interested Bartholdi, since he took care to photograph it. His photograph shows a woman wearing a tunic, her head surrounded by a diadem with seven rays. Pio Fedi also participated in this world's fair, and he could not have failed to notice the work of Elias Robert. This type of crown's symbolism resonated among the French republican reformists; its source is seen in Greco-Roman marble statues of Apollo, the god of music and art, his head encircled by a crown of seven points, symbolizing the Greek Helios, or the Roman Sol—the god of the sun.

"O universal Republic!
You are still only a spark
Tomorrow you will be the
Sun."

— Victor Hugo,"Lux," 1853

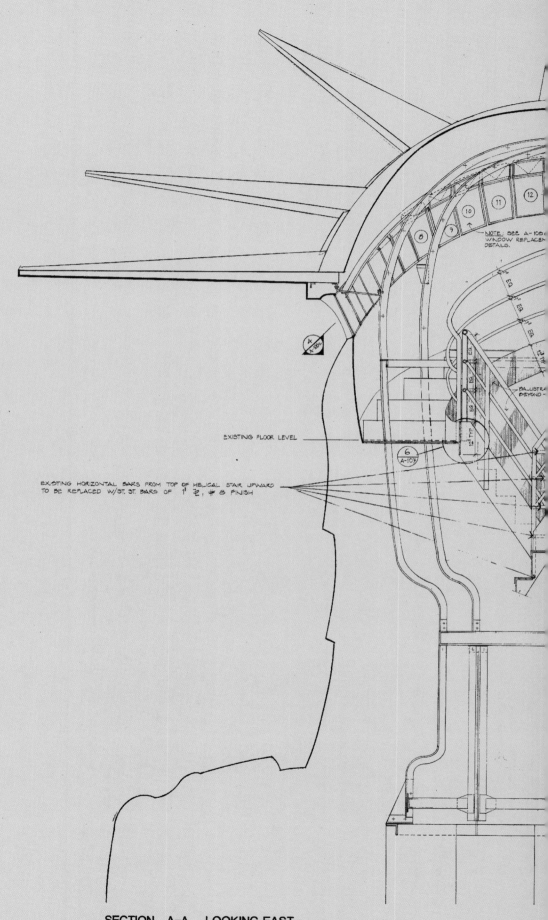

NOTE: SEE A-106 &
WINDOW REPLACEM
DETAILS.

EXISTING FLOOR LEVEL

EXISTING HORIZONTAL BARS FROM TOP OF HELICAL STAIR UPWARD
TO BE REPLACED W/ST. ST. BARS OF 1" $\frac{1}{2}$, # 8 FINISH

SECTION A-A LOOKING EAST

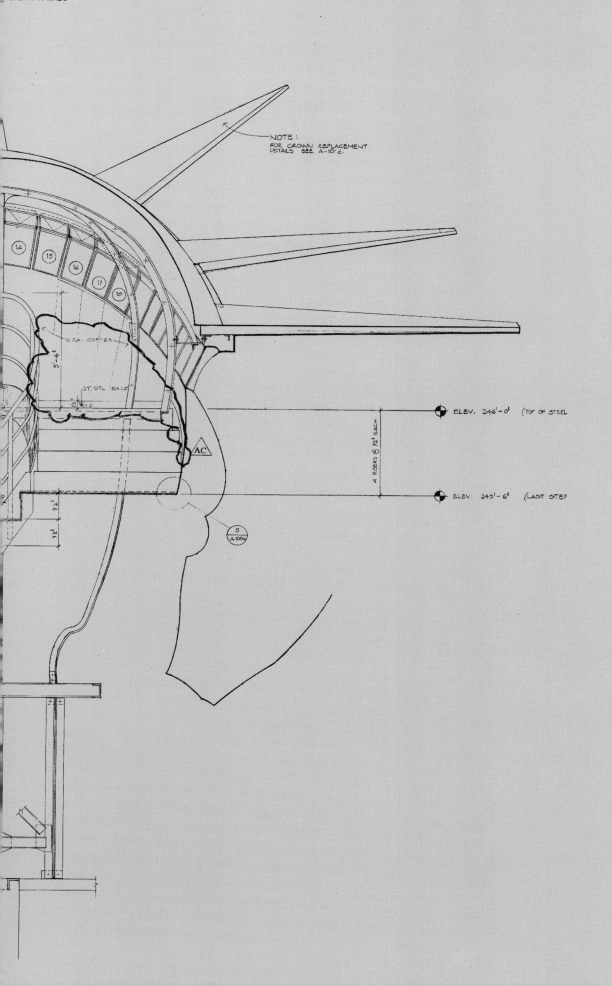

NOTE:
FOR CROWN REPLACEMENT
DETAILS SEE A-10·d.

14 15 16 17 18

16 GA. COPPER

3'-4"

ST. STL BASE

AC

9¾"

9¾"

5
A-100a

ELEV. 246'-0" (TOP OF STEEL

4 RISERS @ 7½" EACH

ELEV. 243'-6" (LAST STEP

"One ascended by a staircase to the dome of the skull and looked out through vacant eyeballs at a bright colored world beneath. I climbed up there often."

— Rudyard Kipling

The sun as a symbol had profound meaning in the French Republic. Since the French Revolution, statues dedicated to republican values have often been styled with a kind of solar halo. The Third French Republic, founded in 1870, used as the state seal the medal created by the engraver Jean-Jacques Barre in 1849: his Republic is a seated woman, wearing a crown of seven points. The poem "Lux" by Victor Hugo, part of his *Les Châtiments* (*Castigations*) criticizing Napoléon III and the restoration of the Empire, speaks to this connection: "O universal Republic! / You are still only a spark / Tomorrow you will be the Sun."

The seven points of the Statue of Liberty's crown have been referred to as symbolizing the seven seas or the seven continents, but research has not confirmed this. However, the allusion to the Masonic sun in Bartholdi's work is clear. Adolphe Crémieux, a friend of Bartholdi's and a member of his Freemason Lodge described "the Great Architect of the Universe [who] gave the sun to the world to illuminate it, and freedom to support it." The sun dispenses light, chasing the shadow of ignorance and the night of false beliefs. This underlies Bartholdi's decision to place upon the Statue's head a crown rather than the Phrygian cap popularized in revolutionary France. In his eyes, the cap linked to bloody insurrection wouldn't have connected his work to the philosophical values that were dear to him.

opposite
The 1986 centennial restoration.

below, right
Photograph, taken by Bartholdi, of the Palais de l'Industrie, 1885 Exposition Universelle, Paris.

below, left
Head of the Statue on display in Paris, 1883.

The symbolism of the sun also radiates from the flame of the torch, the first element of the Statue exhibited to the public, during Philadelphia's 1876 Centennial Exposition. The head of the Statue was next to be shared, at Paris's 1878 Exposition Universelle.

There it became a major attraction because visitors could climb up inside the head to view the houses and streets surrounding the fair. A young Rudyard Kipling, the future author of *The Jungle Book*, noted: "One ascended by a staircase to the dome of the skull and looked out through vacant eyeballs at a bright colored world beneath. I climbed up there often."

Bartholdi had the shrewd idea of reserving access to the Statue's head to visitors who paid a fee. At the completion of their visit, they could then stop at the souvenir stand placed beneath the head to purchase a model of the head in bronze, a printed scarf, an embroidered satin badge, or even a piece of copper stamped with the fair's date. And, of course, people were strongly encouraged to participate in the public subscription, which was helping to finance the construction of the Statue.

Gaining broad public support through subscriptions was part of Bartholdi's commitment to a monument to democracy—and the sign of a savvy promotor. Bartholdi knew how to utilize the power of public opinion. With this monument, Bartholdi brought an ancient symbol to a new, modern age.

Give me your tired,
your huddled mass
breathe free, the wr
your teeming shore
homeless, tempest-
lamp beside the gol

your poor,

es yearning to

etched refuse of

Send these, the

ost to me, I lift my

den door!

Emma Lazarus
"The New Colossus," 1883

An Iconic and Timeless Power

Who could have imagined a giant Statue of Liberty entirely made of Legos? In 2017, celebrated Lego designer Erik Varszegi achieved this feat. A nine-foot-tall replica made of 25,375 of these small bricks was displayed at the Smithsonian's National Museum of American History in Washington D.C., part of the opening of its new wing, themed "The Nation We Build Together." Whether built of Legos or copper, iron, and steel, the Statue is a reminder of how populations from the entire world make up the American people.

The message of the Statue speaks to the world, so it is more than a landmark or a national symbol.
The Statue's universality allows it to be simultaneously a memorial site, a reflection of the passage of time, and a promise for the future. And the myriad representations that the Statue inspires manage to retain this complex and potent message.

In 2011, with the approval of Paris's Conservatoire National des Arts et Métiers, which has the first plaster model of the State of Liberty, art dealer Guillaume Duhamel created a limited edition of twelve bronze reproductions of the Statue, cast by Susse Fondeur. Since its unveiling on June 9, 2011, the first of the twelve bronze replicas has stood at the CNAM museum's entrance. Another of these ten-foot-tall replicas is in New York, standing at the entrance to 667 Madison Avenue.

There are a striking number of Statue of Liberty replicas in the world. Of the "official" ones executed by Bartholdi's casters, there are fourteen in France; one in Lakenheath, Great Britain; one in Birmingham, Alabama; one in Buenos Aires; and one in the suburbs of Rio de Janeiro. This last has engraved upon its tablet "15 de Novembro 1889," the date of the Brazilian military coup d'état that overthrew the constitutional monarchy of emperor Pedro II and established the First Brazilian Republic. (Interestingly, this same date is featured on the small-scale Statue of Liberty model located in Paris's Musée d'Orsay.)

The Statue of Liberty has an extraordinary capacity to echo the concerns of the moment. From the time of its origin, the Statue has inspired political cartoonists. In a comment about American avarice, it appears in Joseph Udo Keppler's 1912 illustration *Golden Cow Replaces Liberty*: the Statue floats in New York Harbor, in distress, because she was replaced by a "golden calf" whose collar features a dollar sign.

During fraught moments in history, the United States government knew how to leverage the Statue's emotional resonance. In 1918, illustrator Joseph Pennel created a government poster that transforms the Statue. Titled *That Liberty Shall Not Perish from the Earth*, it depicts an apocalyptic scene, with the Statue's pedestal on fire, city buildings in ruins, and the sky ablaze with war planes. The poster's message is to buy treasury bonds to finance the U.S. Army's participation in the fighting in Europe. This method was employed again during World War II.

On July 3, 2000, the *New Yorker* published a drawing
by the Canadian artist Anita Kunz on its front page.
Titled *Climber*, the image depicts a person trying to scale
the Statue's nose—showing that there's still progress to
be made in terms of liberty being integrated into society.
The devastation of September 11, 2001, saw countless
depictions of Lady Liberty crying in grief, holding her
head in her hands. Joe Heller, John Sherffius, Corky
Trinidad, Mike Lane, and Henry Payne are just a few
of the great political cartoonists who have used the
likeness of the Statue of Liberty to respond to issues
of the day. Following the 2015 attacks in Paris, even
Google put the Statue in the spotlight, with cartoonist
Dave Granlund depicting the Statue lighting candles.
Engraved on its tablet? The words "Je suis Paris."

The Statue of Liberty's iconic potential is such that
advertisers immediately thought that it was the ideal
monument to render products desirable.
At the beginning of the Statue's existence, even before
it was fully constructed, its image was transformed to
sell lightbulbs, glass, and medications.

"Hello! This Is Liberty Speaking—Billions of Dollars Are Needed Now."

— World War I war bonds campaign

BIRTHDAY

bloomingdales

CRIME ABOVE THE HARBOR

HELLO!
THIS IS LIBERTY SPEAKING—
BILLIONS OF DOLLARS ARE NEEDED
AND NEEDED NOW

SAVE THE AIR
PROTEST
REUSE
CONSERVE
ACT NOW!

EARTH DAY 91 NEW YORK CITY

WILLIAM FOX presents
FOUR SONS
— BIG AS THE HEART OF HUMANITY —
JOHN FORD PRODUCTION

USA 29

CAPTAIN MARVEL JR.
FEB 24 NO. 36
10¢
MASTER COMICS

CAPT. MARVEL JR.
battles
FOR LIBERTY

Fact and Science Fiction
FEBRUARY 50¢
AMAZING stories

BESIDE THE GOLDEN DOOR, by Henry Slesar

BRIDGE TO AZRAEL
Novel by John Brunner

Liberty.
The beautiful.

1886-1986:
Centennial of the
Statue of Liberty and Avon.
100 years of beauty.

SOME THING HAS FOUND US

CLOVERFIELD
01-18-08

Meet Fievel. In his search to find his family, he discovered America.

STEVEN SPIELBERG
AN AMERICAN TAIL
DON BLUTH

FREEDOM OF EXPRESSION
OF RELIGION
FROM WANT
FROM FEAR

1791 — 1941

EVERYWHERE IN THE WORLD
JUNIOR MEMBERS ROUND TABLE PENNSYLVANIA LIBRARY ASSOCIATION
PENNA ART W.P.A.

WNBA
NEW YORK
LIBERTY
NEW YORK
LIBERTY

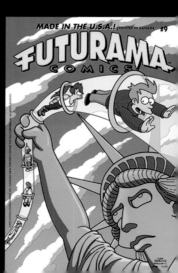

MADE IN THE U.S.A.! (PRINTED IN CANADA) #9
FUTURAMA COMICS

LIBERTY
1886 CENTENNIAL 1986

KEEP THE TORCH LIT™

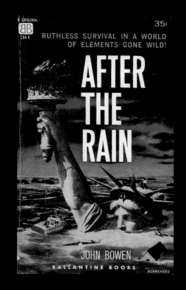

RUTHLESS SURVIVAL IN A WORLD OF ELEMENTS GONE WILD!

AFTER THE RAIN

JOHN BOWEN

BALLANTINE BOOKS

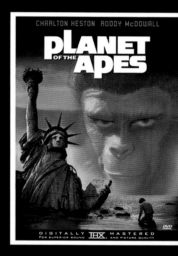

CHARLTON HESTON · RODDY McDOWALL

PLANET OF THE APES

Levi's

FROM THE DIRECTOR OF INDEPENDENCE DAY

THE DAY AFTER TOMORROW

MAY 28 · WHERE WILL YOU BE?

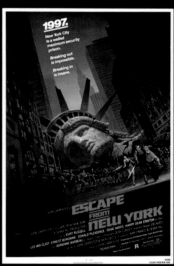

1997.

ESCAPE FROM NEW YORK

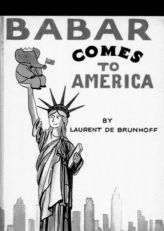

BABAR COMES TO AMERICA

BY LAURENT DE BRUNHOFF

Next Stop... New Jersey

NCAA FINAL FOUR
1996 · MEADOWLANDS

Mr. Potato Head

VENTURA COUNTY · LEMONS

ONWARD

LIFE
AMERICA THE WONDROUS

Gillette
LE RASOIR DE SURETE

Many large American brands have appropriated the image of the Statue of Liberty, from Levi's and Hollywood gum to Coca-Cola, a brand that has the same birth year as the Statue. A French truck company, Willème, didn't hesitate to use it as an emblem. *V* magazine dared to compare Lady Gaga to Lady Liberty. Countless products that have used its image could have had a negative effect. But the Statue's message of liberation remains potent, with democratic protestors around the world utilizing it, such as when Tiananmen Square protestors adopted the Statue as a mascot in 1989.

In an instance of art creating art, the Statue of Liberty lends its power to other works of art. Andy Warhol incorporated the Statue in various works, paying homage to its modernity. The Taiwanese painter Tsing-Fang Chen made a series in the 1980s around the concept of "neo-iconography art," integrating the statue as a motif into very well-known works by artists like Henri Matisse, Marc Chagall, and Vincent van Gogh. In one painting of his, *City Gleaners* (1985), Paul Gauguin's nude bathers contemplate Jean-François Millet's gleaners, who pick up used cans of popular drinks at the foot of the Statue of Liberty.

The Statue of Liberty is present in all forms of art, including music and drama—such as Irving Berlin's successful musical comedy *Miss Liberty*, created for Broadway in 1949. In it, a newspaper publisher tells a reporter to find Bartholdi's muse—even then people wondered who had modeled for the Statue.

Novelists make the Statue a character, a setting, a memory, or a symbol. John Bowen's 1958 novel *After the Rain* portrays the Statue absorbed by raging floods brought on by a natural disaster. In Paul Auster's *Leviathan*, published in 1992, the main character, Benjamin Sachs, blows up replicas of the Statue around the country to denounce the abuses of American power.

below
An illustration for *Lucky Luke*.

opposite
Keith Haring's monumental banner "CityKids Speak on Liberty" was created in conjunction with The CityKids Foundation to commemorate the centennial anniversary of the Statue of Liberty's arrival in the United States, in 1986.

"You're not just the symbol of a statue that we love, but the most beautiful girl in the world."

— Irving Berlin

The covers of 1930s pulp magazines like *Astounding Stories of Super Science* thrilled readers by depicting attacks against New York and the Statue. Comics also showed the Statue prominently, sometimes critical of its symbolism, such as 2009's *Universal War 1, Revelations #1* by Denis Bajram. Modern video games like *Command & Conquer – Red Alert* and *Crysis 3* often place the Statue in a position to be saved.

Since its beginnings, cinema has adopted the Statue as part of the scene or as a symbol. The first movie to feature it might have been *The Immigrant* by Charlie Chaplin, in 1917. Since then, cinemagoers have seen the Statue take a role in movies as far-ranging as *Saboteur* by Alfred Hitchcock (1942), *Planet of the Apes* (1967), *X-Men* (2000), and *2012: Ice Age* (2011).

As well-engineered as the Statue of Liberty is, in movies it can be destroyed by nature, humans, or even extraterrestrials. In one of the first American science fiction movies, *Deluge* (1933), directed by Felix E. Feist, a natural disaster devastates the Pacific Coast of the United States, eventually reaching the East Coast and destroying New York. For the first time people witnessed a shocking loss of the Statue of Liberty, carried away by monstrous waves. *The Day After Tomorrow* (2004) and *Cloverfield* (2008) are in the same vein. But within the Statue's cinematic, often apocalyptic deaths, invariably there is a kind of revival. Despite the most over-the-top fictional fate, and despite being parodied and sanctified, appropriated and commercialized, the Statue of Liberty remains a timeless emblem of the United States, a totem of humanity and its dream.

VOL. LXIV. No. 1645.   PUCK BUILDING, New York, September 9th, 1908.   PRICE TEN CENTS.

"What Fools these Mortals be!"

Puck

IF BRONZE COULD CHANGE!

The Centennial Restoration: Rebuilding the Face of Liberty

In 2017, nearly four and a half million visitors explored the Statue of Liberty, the pedestal, and the grounds of Liberty Island. The Statue attracted visitors as soon as it was assembled on Bedloe's Island. In 1890, eighty-eight thousand people came to the island. In 1945, there were five hundred thousand; in 1964, a milestone was reached with one million visitors. Today, back-and-forth ferries for the Statue's millions of visitors are effortlessly synchronized. Manicured lawns border the Statue's pedestal. The Statue has been restored and is stronger than ever. A brand-new, freestanding museum introduces visitors to the history of the site and monument. It's a park that combines the beauty of New York Harbor and the legacy of one of the world's most famous statues, all under the protection of the National Park Service. Time, money, and willpower were needed to get to this point.

The unveiling of the Statue of Liberty, on October 28, 1886, was a moment of extraordinary international cooperation. But a new, hidden challenge was brewing: how to maintain and protect this monument. Sited on an island in the middle of New York's harbor, the Statue was exposed to salt water, rain, wind, and extremes of cold and heat. Questions soon arose: How should the Statue be protected? And, how would this be paid for?

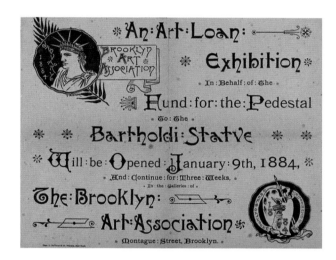

"One of the most successful public-private partnerships in U.S. history."

— Stephen A. Briganti

Since the Statue's conception, Bartholdi and Laboulaye wanted its financing to come directly from the people, not from the government. Public subscription was considered the right democratic touch, and the French would finance the Statue, while the Americans would be responsible for the pedestal. However, on both sides of the Atlantic, subscription efforts were slow to raise money—not everyone understood the importance of the monument or how beautiful it would be. That the pedestal was indeed funded by so many small donors is due to the initiative of Joseph Pulitzer, the publisher of *The World* newspaper, although most of the financing came from several generous donors.

After the Statue's installment on Bedloe's Island, the responsibility for its upkeep and arrangements for visitors fell to a range of entities. The Statue was initially maintained by the federally managed U.S. Lighthouse Board. The American Committee, who had helped raise funds to finance the pedestal, managed the ferry boats for visitors. The State of New York and New York City were not involved. Even after the Statue's dedication, the island was a functioning military base, although there was a stand selling hot dogs and souvenirs. (The same family still operates the food and gift shop on the island today.)

Lawmakers were reluctant from the beginning to commit funds to finance the Statue. In 1877, when Congress officially accepted France's gift, Pennsylvania Senator Simon Cameron assured his colleagues by saying that it "wouldn't cost a penny." In 1890, the Senate blocked a law looking to transform the island into a public park— the Federal government's priority at that time was to build a new immigration inspection station. Ellis Island opened in 1892.

With minimal funding and a lack of strong oversight,
damage to the Statue soon began to escalate.
The lighting system within the Statue desperately
needed upgrades. Leaking water corroded the internal
structure. Traces of rust stained the monument. By the
beginning of the twentieth century, journalists started
using the word "shame" when referring to the Statue.

This kind of critical public sentiment brought a renewed
focus to Bartholdi's creation. On October 15, 1924, the
Statue was declared a National Monument by President
Calvin Coolidge; however, no new funding was allocated.
Finally, in the wake of the New Deal following the
financial crisis of 1929, President Franklin Roosevelt
made federal funding available for the Statue. Bedloe's
Island was wholly placed under the jurisdiction of the
National Park Service.

The Statue's fiftieth anniversary, in 1936, was an occasion
for Roosevelt to recall immigrants' contributions to
the United States' success: "For over three centuries a
steady stream of men, women, and children followed the
beacon of liberty which this light symbolizes.
They brought to us strength and moral fiber developed
in a civilization centuries old but fired anew by the
dream of a better life in America. They brought to one
new country the cultures of a hundred old ones."

PENNSYLVANIA   11 SUBMARINE D TYPE   13 ARMOURED CRUISER SAN DIEGO   16 ARMOURED CRUISER PITTSBURGH   21 BATTLE SHIP NEBRASKA
ISLAND   12 SUPERDREADNAUGHT NEW YORK   14 BATTLE SHIP MASSACHUSETTS   17 LATEST BATTLE CRUISER   22 ARMOURED CRUISER NORTH CAROLINA
UTAH   15 BATTLE SHIP VIRGINIA   18 PROTECTED CRUISER OLYMPIA   23 ARMOURED CRUISER PUEBLO
TEXAS   19 SUPERDREADNAUGHT MISSISSIPPI   24 MONITOR OZARK
UNCLE SAM'S BIG FIGHTING SHIPS   20 BATTLE SHIP ILLINOIS   25 ARMOURED CRUISER SEATTLE

Under the auspices of the Works Progress Administration (WPA), in 1938 a vast maintenance and construction plan was put in place, which included demolishing the old military buildings, replacing the cast-iron steps with concrete ones, planting trees, and leveling the grounds. Then, after World War II, Congress passed appropriations to fund construction of the public pier, new ferry lines, and buildings for the National Park Service administration. In 1956, Bedloe's Island was renamed Liberty Island, and in 1965, President Johnson made Ellis Island part of the National Park Service, to be administered under the Statue of Liberty National Monument.

With the Statue's one-hundredth anniversary approaching in 1986, stakes grew higher. While maintenance and management of the Statue and the island were federally funded, the monument had fallen into serious disrepair due to the large number of visitors and structural problems that dated back to the original construction. A global restoration strategy, which would include Ellis Island, needed to be initiated and financed. In 1981, a joint French and American committee began to work with the National Park Service to develop an architectural and engineering report on the physical condition of the Statue, make recommendations for restoration work, and develop a detailed feasibility study.

However, it became apparent that the committee was not capable of doing the considerable fundraising and overall management that this important project required.

In 1982, President Reagan established a public commission to study the committee's plan and designated Lee A. Iacocca to preside over it. As a son of Italian immigrants and a successful automobile executive, Iacocca had become the face of American ingenuity. At Ford Motor Company, Iacocca had been instrumental in the development and promotion of the Mustang. As president and chairman of the board of Chrysler Corporation, he was credited with reviving the company and saving it from bankruptcy.

Under Iacocca's direction, The Statue of Liberty-Ellis Island Foundation, Inc., was created to raise the funds and manage the project. Iacocca encouraged contributions from all Americans and corporate donors such as Coca-Cola, Kellogg, Stroh Brewery, American Airlines, Oscar Mayer, and Avon. Just as Bartholdi had raised money by selling souvenirs at the Philadelphia Centennial Exposition in 1876 and the 1878 Exposition Universelle in Paris, almost one hundred companies were given permission to use the likeness of the Statue of Liberty on products as varied as T-shirts, sweaters, ashtrays, charcoal lighters, and air fresheners. Special commemorative coins and stamps were created that included the Statue's image, with the coins themselves raising $84 million for the project.

below

In 1982, President Ronald Reagan asked Lee A. Iacocca, president and chairman of Chrysler Corporation, to head a private sector effort to raise funds for the restoration and preservation of the Statue of Liberty and Ellis Island.

One of Iacocca's key decisions was to recruit a young man of Italian heritage to lead the Foundation: Stephen A. Briganti. As president of the Foundation, Briganti has coordinated the redevelopment of the main building on Ellis Island into the National Museum of Immigration and the creation of the new Statue of Liberty Museum. A part of the restoration of the monument and its transition into the twenty-first century, Briganti forged the conditions for a harmonious relationship between the Foundation and the National Park Service: "One of the most successful public-private partnership in U.S. history," he's said. Since its creation, the Foundation has raised nearly $1 billion and Liberty and Ellis Islands were transformed.

For Iacocca and his restoration team, the process began with a review of the technical problems that had been identified by the Franco-American team. The damage was worse than expected.

"This colossal statue is a masterpiece of the human spirit."

—UNESCO

The Statue's head and right shoulder were misaligned—
the head two feet off from center and the right arm
eighteen inches from the body. This had probably been
the case since the Statue had been assembled on the
island. The torch and a part of the arm also hadn't been
constructed according to the initial plans. Beneath the
Statue's dress, extensive damage was uncovered. To
make the repairs, a self-supported aluminum scaffolding
had to be built around the whole Statue without touching
any part of the copper skin. To reach the crown and
torch, an exterior elevator was built on the scaffolding.

Improvements were more than skin deep. The interior
iron framework created by Eiffel linking the copper
skin and the skeleton was reconstructed in stainless
steel. Teflon-based insulation was placed between the
individual steel bars and the copper skin; as the original
insulation failed, the original iron bars had come
into contact with the copper, causing the iron bars to
deteriorate. The rivets were replaced, and the shoulder
repaired.

The head's frame was repositioned in alignment with the
central pylon, and the twenty-five windows in the crown
were replaced. The anchoring system at the pedestal's
interior was reinforced. Innovations included an interior
space reorganized around a new staircase and double-
decker elevators.

A new lighting system in the interior of the Statue
showcased the incredible technical details that allowed
it to stand. Two bronze doors with bas-reliefs provided
easy access to visitors. Ventilation and cooling systems
were installed, adding to the comfort of visitors.

opposite and below
The old torch being removed from the Statue during
the 1986 centennial restoration.

The most serious problem uncovered was the dilapidated
state of the torch, its flame severely damaged by water. It
was decided not to restore this torch but instead create
an exact replica, this time gilding the embossed copper
flame with gold leaf in accordance with Bartholdi's
original plans. A dozen French artisans specializing
in repoussé from the renowned metalworks firm Les
Métalliers Champenois were tasked with this restoration.
The removal of the old flame from the top of the Statue
merited a public ceremony, which took place on July 4,
1984. Today, the Statue's original torch is exhibited in the
new museum, so everyone can visit this priceless piece
of American history.

Also in 1984, the same year that scaffolding wrapped
around the Statue, the Statue of Liberty was designated
a World Heritage site under UNESCO, recognizing the
Statue's "exceptional universal value." In 1986, restoration
was completed in time for the Statue of Liberty to
celebrate a well-deserved one hundredth birthday.

The Museum and Celebrating Liberty for Future Generations

Liberty Island, the home of a unique world monument, now welcomes visitors to its new Statue of Liberty Museum. After the closing of the immigration center on Ellis Island in 1954, the idea for a museum on Liberty Island that would explore the history of immigration in the United States began to be discussed. A number of proposals were developed and rejected in turn as groups debated how to address appropriately the complex subject of immigration and the Statue's connection to it. Finally, after nearly twenty years of discussion, the American Museum of Immigration, housed in the pedestal of the Statue of Liberty, was inaugurated by President Richard Nixon on September 27, 1972.

After the immigration center's closure, Ellis Island itself became the subject of debate. Should it be sold? Should it be turned into an attraction park or a monument?

In 1965, Ellis Island became part of the National Park Service and just a few years later, Congress approved a budget for the preservation and maintenance of the buildings. The opening of the island to the public, in the spring of 1976, encouraged support for the creation of an Ellis Island immigration museum. In 1990, a museum opened within the Main Building, under the fundraising and oversight of The Statue of Liberty-Ellis Island Foundation, working with the National Park Service.

"Lady Liberty is the symbol of everything America is about: freedom, hope, possibility, and resilience."

— Diane von Furstenberg

The Statue of Liberty's centennial attracted attention to Liberty Island. A new permanent exhibition opened in 1986 within the space formerly occupied by the American Museum of Immigration, which focused on the monument's history and featured one hundred objects and documents that illustrated the history and significance of the Statue.
Visitors got to know the Statue's creator, Frédéric-Auguste Bartholdi, and his circle, and art and advertisements showed the tremendous power of the Statue's image around the world.

Unfortunately, this museum was not able to accommodate the many visitors to Liberty Island, sometimes close to twenty-seven thousand a day. After the terrorist attacks on September 11, 2001, admittance to both the pedestal, where the museum was located, and the Statue was regulated more strictly. Still, it soon became clear that the current infrastructure could not hold the number of people who wanted to visit the museum. In addition, the original torch, located in the entrance hall of the pedestal, was not accessible to every visitor. Little by little, the idea of doing better—or at least doing something differently—took hold.

Circumstances played a role in launching the development of a new museum. As a symbol of freedom, the Statue can easily be a terrorist target, and Liberty Island was closed after September 11, 2001 until December 1 of that year. Slowly the Statue opened again to visitors: the pedestal in 2004, and the crown in 2009. Out of these space constraints and circumstances emerged the idea of a separate museum building, offering visitors another experience of the Statue of Liberty. But the lack of available space on the small island made this proposal seem improbable.

Then came Hurricane Sandy. On October 29, 2012, the storm submerged three-quarters of Liberty Island and badly damaged its buildings, although the Statue was unscathed. Once again, the site needed to be closed—this time until July of the next year. Soon thereafter, the decision was made to create a new museum on Liberty Island dedicated to the Statue of Liberty, which would open its doors in 2019. The planning for both the physical structure and museum content involved hundreds of hours by the Foundation, its History Committee, and the National Park Service.

"From building Lady Liberty's pedestal in the 1880s to contributing to the 1986 centennial restoration—the American people have given whatever they could afford to support the Statue."

— Albert C. Bellas, Chairman,
The Statue of Liberty-Ellis Island
Foundation, Inc.

The next task was to secure financing. To chair
the fundraising initiative, Stephen A. Briganti, the
president and CEO of The Statue of Liberty-Ellis Island
Foundation, wanted someone who embodied all facets
of the Statue of Liberty experience. He saw this in
a French-speaking woman from Belgium who had
immigrated to the United States: Diane von Furstenberg,
the media-savvy fashion designer with a global brand.
von Furstenberg is familiar with the price of freedom.
Her mother, a Belgian resistance member who had
been held in Nazi camps during World War II, often said
to her: "You are my torch, my flag of freedom." Being
born in 1946 into a devastated, postwar Europe marks a
person. Much of her drive stems from this experience—
reflected in the title of her memoir *The Woman I Wanted
to Be*. The choice of a woman as chair also served to right
an injustice of the Statue's 1886 inauguration, when not
a single woman apart from a few wives of participating
dignitaries had been allowed on the island.

Von Furstenberg took on the mission to enlist support for
this important endeavor. French-American artist
Anh Duong was commissioned to sculpt fifty stars;
donors could secure these and have their name or
someone they were honoring placed on them.
The Liberty Star mural can be found at the museum's
entrance, a panoramic evocation of freedom composed of
the stylized stars purchased by donors and the "stripes"—
the iron armature bars removed from the Statue during
the centennial restoration. The stars reference not only
the American flag, but also one of the early ideas for the
Statue that Bartholdi had explored, in which he placed
stars instead of windows beneath the crown.

The Statue of Liberty-Ellis Island Foundation mobilized
an unprecedented campaign that would have made
Bartholdi proud, including social media and e-mail
blasts, a crowdfunding effort, and the construction site's
metamorphosis showcased on the Foundation website.
Donations came pouring in, with tens of thousands of
small donors joining the world's leading foundations and
significant philanthropists to support the Foundation's
mission—including many symbolic contributions of
$18.86, marking the year of the inauguration of the Statue.
The campaign was a success, raising $100 million dollars
for island beautification and the new museum. One
hundred and thirty years ago, people from all walks of life
contributed to the realization of the Statue. Clearly, in the
twenty-first century, the same dedication, generosity, and
belief in the ideals of liberty continue to flourish.

p. 188-189
Architectural drawings of the Museum and public
spaces around it.

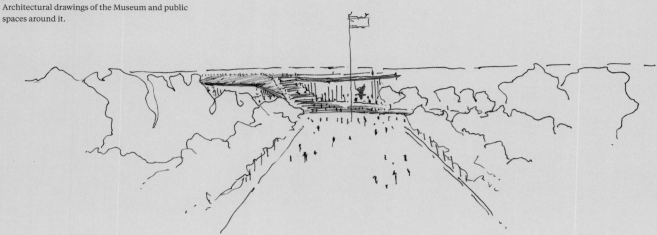

Architect Nicholas Garrison sought to merge the landscape and the building to create a harmonious flow, hence a green roof, a rain garden, and a large window offering views of the original torch's exterior—all within a small half-acre footprint.

Creating a welcoming and user-friendly space, the staircases allow access from the entrance terrace to the rooftop observation deck, which offers spectacular views of the island, the port, and the city—and of course the Statue of Liberty. Complementing the existing structures, the museum's height is no higher than the top of Fort Wood and the pedestal's base. Linking the past to the present, the pleasingly asymmetrical building features bronze and copper, as well as Stony Creek granite, the same stone chosen by Richard Morris Hunt, the architect of the pedestal.

"From the start, the design of the Statue of Liberty museum was conceived as an extension of the park... The island's landscape is lifted and merged with the architecture to create space for the museum in a new geology. The building's angular forms and spaces are shaped by its views and the irregularity of the water's edge, celebrating liberty."

— Nicholas Garrison, FX Collaborative

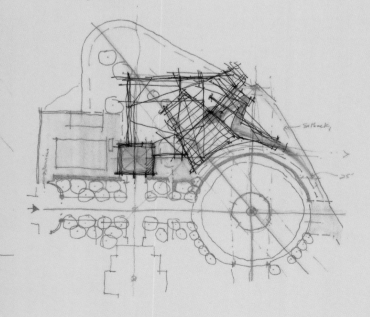

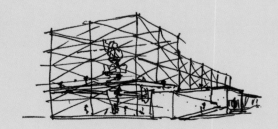

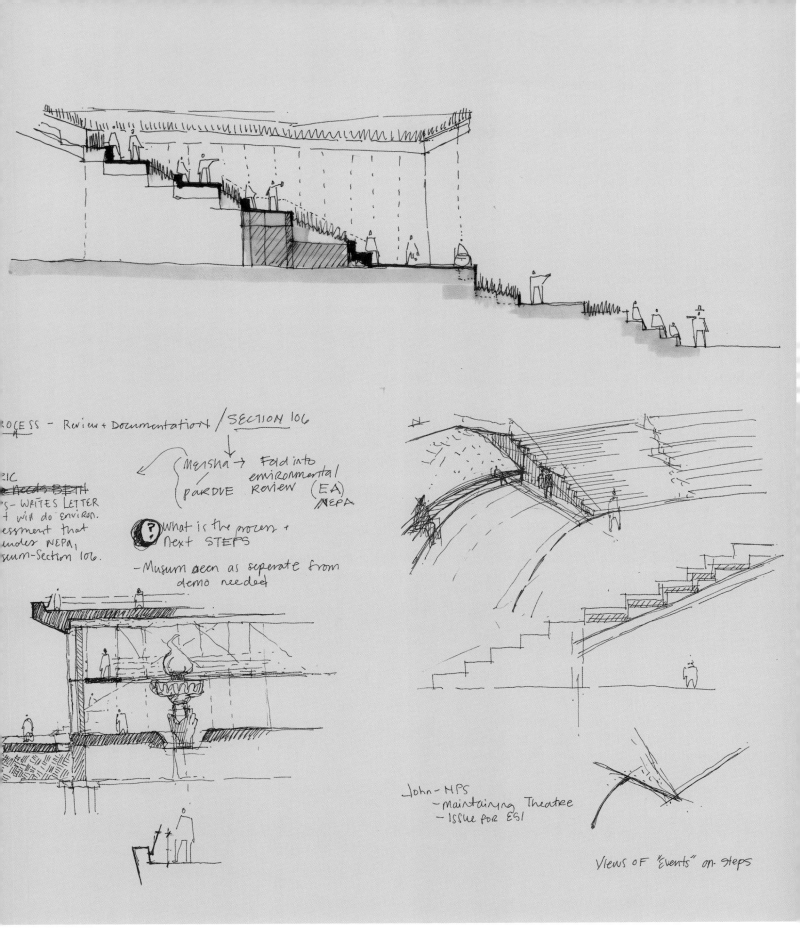

PROCESS - Review + Documentation / SECTION 106

Meisha → Fold into
Pardue environmental Review (EA)
NEPA

? What is the process + Next STEPS

- Musum seen as seperate from demo needed

?IC
Needs BETH
?S - WRITES LETTER
t will do environ.
essment that
nder NEPA,
sum-Section 106.

John - NPS
- maintaining Theatre
- issue for ESI

Views of "Events" on steps

below
Time-lapse photography of the Museum construction, 2013–19.

opposite
Artist's rendering of the Museum's torch enclosure as seen from the terrace.

following spread
The Museum under construction.

pp. 194–195
Artist's rendering of an aerial view of the Museum's torch enclosure and public terrace.

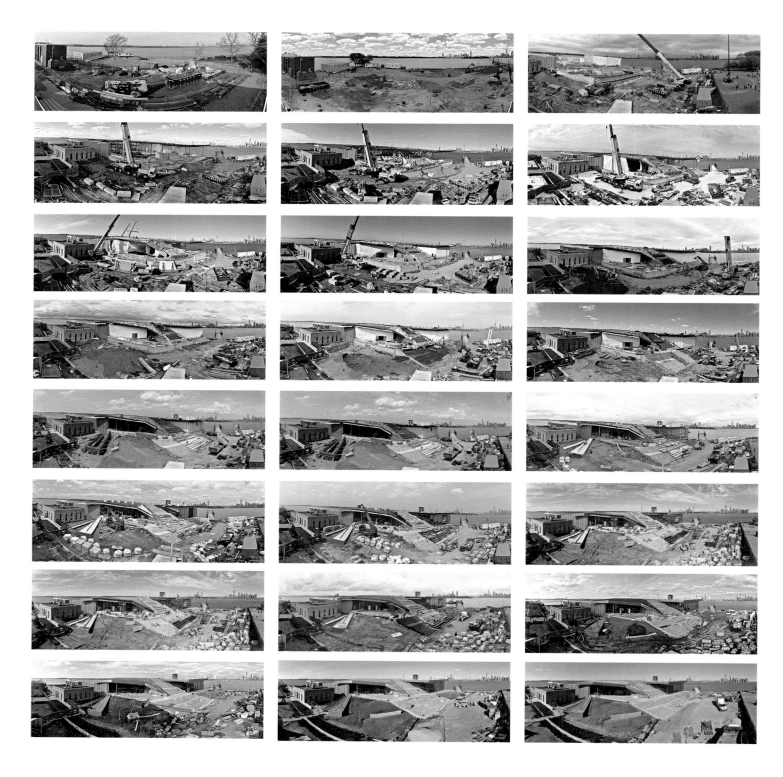

THE MUSEUM AND CELEBRATING LIBERTY FOR FUTURE GENERATIONS

THE MUSEUM AND CELEBRATING LIBERTY FOR FUTURE GENERATIONS

The interior of the space, designed by Edwin Schlossberg, resonates with the idea of discovery. A pioneer of interactive exhibition design, he focused on participatory experiences to convey the rich story of the Statue of Liberty. The Immersive Theater plunges visitors into Bartholdi's era, where they meet the characters of the Statue's incredible adventure. Innovative film and digital tools play with spectacular changes in scale so that visitors feel as though they are within the Statue. Among the artifacts and interactive multimedia in the Engagement Gallery, visitors delve into the technical production process of the Statue and the pedestal and discover how the monument has been adopted as a symbol, from civil rights movements to the arts.

In a huge, moving mosaic of evolving images that merges visitors into the museum narrative, the Inspiration Gallery brings each person back to the present time to ask, "What does Liberty mean to me?" The tour ends at Liberty's original torch—a magical moment in which the viewer comes face-to-face with the greatest symbol of Frédéric-Auguste Bartholdi's oeuvre. There visitors are able to contemplate Bartholdi's flame—and its message—while gazing at the Flag Pole Plaza and the Statue of Liberty.

The new museum inspires one to reflect on this monument to freedom, which became a powerful beacon of hope for immigrants and people around the world. It evokes liberty as an ideal—one that people are finding more precious than ever before. It shows that the present owes much to the long history of this monument. And it demonstrates that the Statue of Liberty's monumental dream is alive and will continue to change and evolve.

Donors
Acknowledgment

Corporate Sponsor

Liberty Mutual Insurance

Liberty Star Club

Allen & Company
American Express
Anonymous
Apple
The Bezos Family
Bloomberg Philanthropies
The Charles Cahn Family
Carnegie Corporation of New York
Chanel, Inc.
The Coca-Cola Foundation
Comcast NBCUniversal
The James and Judith Dimon Foundation
Michael and Linda Donovan
Massimo Ferragamo
The Diller-von Furstenberg Family Foundation
David Geffen Foundation
Jeffrey and Paula Gural
The Hess Family
Judy and Peter Blum Kovler Foundation
The Lauder Foundation
The Ralph and Ricky Lauren Family Foundation
Mellody Hobson and George Lucas
Mr. Frank McCourt
Deborah Simon
Stavros Niarchos Foundation
The Tisch Family
The Walt Disney Company

Torch Club

DeWalt
Ford Foundation
GRoW @ Annenberg Foundation
The Hearst Foundation, Inc.

Crown Club

Aryeh and Elana Bourkoff
Sergey Brin
Charina Endowment Fund
The Gabelli Family Foundation
The Howard and Abby Milstein Family

Independence Club

ABC News and Walt Disney Imagineering
David Bonderman & Dr. Laurie Michaels
Brian Cury, EarthCam, Inc.
Tina Santi Flaherty
History Channel
The Family of Eugene & Phyllis McGovern and Pavarini
  McGovern LLC
NYC & Company Foundation
Phelps Construction Group
Unilumin North America
Yap Studios

Pedestal Club

Alex and Ani
Mr. and Mrs. Albert C. Bellas
Richard H. Brown and Jane S. Brown
Rachel & Maxime Haot
Gedale D. Horowitz
Liberty Ambassadors, LLC
Mutual of America, Your Retirement Company
The New York Community Trust
Samuel Freeman Charitable Trust
Shinola Detroit
Tiffany & Co.

Freedom Club

A.P. Kirby, Jr. Foundation, Inc.
Back Brook Masonry
Peter and Eileen Lehrer
The Supor Family
Turnpike Electric Inc.
Judith Rodin and Paul Verkuil

Statue of Liberty-Ellis Island Foundation, Inc.

Partners Acknowledgment

Architect
FXCollaborative

Nicholas Garrison
Sylvia Smith
Ann Rolland
Daniel Piselli
Nicholas Cates
Ilana Judah
Kazuhiro Adachi
Miwa Fukui
James Bushong
J. Cameron Ringness
Stephen Scribner
James Theodore
Patrick Koch
Pascale Sablan
Shalini Abeyaratne
Brandon Massey
Alp Bozkurt

Project Management
SBI Consultants

Wajdi Atallah
James Grogg
Nina Arron
Rosa Melillo

Construction Manager
Phelps Construction Group

Douglas G. Phelps, *President*
Jeffrey Rainforth, *Vice President*
Tom Brennan, *Project Manager*
Richard Lemere, *Chief Estimator*
Stacey O'Leary, *Chief Financial Officer*
Amanda Joinson, *Contract Administrator*
Christopher LaPointe, *Assistant Project Manager*
Lawrence Sidoti, *General Superintendent*
Anthony Stefanacci, *Project Superintendent*
James Giannetti Jr., *Superintendent*
Dennis Hastie, *Superintendent*

Exhibits
ESI Design

Edwin Schlossberg, *Principal*
Presston Brown, *Project Manager*
Emily Webster Bağdatli, *Design Lead*
Laura Gunther, *Graphic Designer*
Matt Weisgerber, *Physical Designer*
Charles Deluga, *Systems Designer*
Nick Hubbard, *Content Designer*
Clay Gish, *Content Designer*
Caroline Bevan Rojek, *Media Producer*
Sarah Frankel, *Production Manager*
Trip Kyle, *Production Manager*
Jonathan Grimm, *Art Director*
Tarley Jordan, *Marketing & Communications*
Yuri Sunahara, *Interaction Designer*
Gideon D'Arcangelo, *Creative Strategy*
Alexandra Alfaro, *Design Management*
Amanda Pietropaolo, *Media Coordinator*
Debra Everett-Lane, *Content Designer*
Joe Karadin, *Physical Designer*

Further Reading

Agulhon, Maurice. *Marianne into Battle: Republican Imagery and Symbolism in France, 1789–1880*, Cambridge, UK: Cambridge University Press, 1981.

Andinder, Tyler. *City of Dreams: The 400-Year Epic History of Immigrant New York*. Boston: Houghton Mifflin Harcourt, 2016.

Baker, Paul R. *Richard Morris Hunt*. Cambridge, MA: MIT Press, 1980.

Belot, Robert. *Bartholdi. L'homme qui inventa la Liberté*. Paris: Ellipse, 2019.

Berenson, Edward. *The Statue of Liberty: A Transatlantic Story*. New Haven, CT: Yale University Press, 2012.

Bermond, Daniel. *Gustave Eiffel*. Paris: Perrin, 2002.

Boime, Albert. *Hollow Icons: The Politics of Sculpture in Nineteenth-Century France, Kent, Ohio, and London*. Kent, OH: The Kent State University Press, 1987.

Boime, Albert. *The Unveiling of the National Icons: A Plea for Patriotic Iconoclasm in a Nationalist Era*. Cambridge, UK, Cambridge University Press, 1998.

Darnton, Robert. *Mesmerism and the End of the Enlightenment in France*. Cambridge, MA: Harvard University Press, 1968.

Gray, Walter Dennis. *Interpreting American Democracy in France: The Career of Édouard Laboulaye, 1811–1883*. Plainsboro, NJ: Associated University Presses, 1994.

Grote, Harriet. *Memoir of the Life of Ary Scheffer*. London: John Murray, 1860.

Hackett Fischer, David, *Liberty and Freedom: A Visual History of America's Founding Ideas*. New York: Oxford University Press, 2004.

Hargrove, June Ellen, and Pierre Provoyeur, ed. *Liberty: The French-American Statues in Art and History*. New York Public Library and Comité Officiel Franco-Américain pour la Célébration du Centenaire. New York: HarperCollins, 1986.

Harvie, David I. *Eiffel: The Genius Who Reinvented Himself*. Gloucestershire, UK: The History Press, 2005.

Jennings, Lawrence C. *French Anti-Slavery: The Movement for the Abolition of Slavery in France, 1802–1848*. Cambridge, UK: Cambridge University Press, 2000.

Khan, Yasmin Sabin, *Enlightening the World: The Creation of the Statue of Liberty*. Ithaca, NY: Cornell University Press, 2010.

Kramer, Lloyd S. *Lafayette in Two Worlds: Public Cultures and Personal Identities in an Age of Revolutions*. Chapel Hill: University of North Carolina Press, 1999.

Lefebvre, René (Édouard de Laboulaye). *Paris in America*. Translated by Mary L. Booth. New York: Charles Scribner, 1863.

Mitchell, Elizabeth. *Liberty's Torch: The Great Adventure to Build the Statue of Liberty*. New York: Grove Press, 2014.

Moreno, Barry. *The Statue of Liberty Encyclopedia*. New York: Simon & Schuster, 2000.

Seitz, Don C. *Joseph Pulitzer: His Life and Letters*. New York: Simon and Schuster, 1924.

Trachtenberg, Marvin. *The Statue of Liberty*. New York: Viking Press, 1966.

Credits

Aerial images provided by FlyNYON.

146, 147 (Alamy Stock Photo)
170-171 (Barbara Alper)
10 (Peter Arnell)
152-153, 180, 185 (Fenton Bailey/ World of Wonder Productions)
16, 17, 20, 51, 53, 66, 67, 70-71, 78, 80, 100, 115, 116 (Bartholdi Museum, Colmar, Reproduction © Christian Kempf)
15, 61 (Bartholdi Museum, Colmar, Photo © Christian Kempf)
24, 27, 39, 43, 50, 53, 55, 59, 65, 70, 71, 79, 104, 108, 111, 115, 127, 132, 135 (Robert Belot)
176-177, 178-179 (© Richard Berenholtz)
114 (Neal Boenzi/The New York Times)
6 (Diane Bondareff / AP Images for Statue of Liberty-Ellis Island Foundation)
146 (Bongo Comics)
41 (Noel Y. Calingasan @ nyclovesnyc)
151 (The CityKids Foundation, © Keith Haring Foundation)
146 (Cooper Hewitt Smithsonian Design Museum)
118-119, 174 (© Dan Cornish/Esto)
130-131 (© Dan Cornish/ National Park Service)
190 (Brian Cury and EarthCam, Inc.)

191, 194-195, 196-197, 199 (© FXCollaborative)
22-23, 43, 49, 51, 79, 86, 100, 102, 103, 106-107, 124-125, 133, 141, 144, 146, 182-183 (Getty Images)
149 (© Bob Gruen / www.bobgruen. com)
146, 151 (Keith Haring Foundation)
147 (Houghton Mifflin Harcourt)
14, 156-157 (Jamie Huenefeld)
64 (Kelly Kopp @newyorkcitykopp)
4-5 (Dan Kurtzman)
147 (Levi Strauss & Co.)
24, 30, 36, 39, 40, 42, 47, 92, 93, 99, 135, 146, 155 (Library of Congress Prints and Photographs Division, Washington, D.C.)
150 (LUCKY LUKE 8 – UN COW-BOY A PARIS © LUCKY COMICS 2019 by Jul & Achdé d'après Morris)
146 (Marvel Entertainment LLC)
87 (© Musée des arts et métiers-CNAM, Paris / photo S. Pelly)
34 (Museum of the City of New York)
147 (NCAA)
89, 166 (National Archives, Washington, D.C.)
9, 11, 28-29, 48, 52, 58, 60, 62-63, 69, 76, 77, 90-91, 94, 95, 96, 97, 113, 120-121, 128-129, 134, 146, 147, 161, 164-165, 169, 175, 184, 186, 188, 189, 199 (National Park Service / The Statue of Liberty-Ellis Island Foundation, Inc.)

146 (National Portrait Gallery, © Guy Rene Billout)
18, 24, 26, 38, 159 (Manuscripts and Archives Division, The New York Public Library)
27 (Niday Picture Library / Alamy Stock Photo)
122-123 (Koni Nordmann/Focus-Agentur)
148 (© Denis Ouch)
147 (Penguin Random House)
142-143 (Property of a Private Collection)
Cover, Back Cover, 2-3, 37, 56-57, 72, 73, 81, 82-83, 84, 88, 98, 101, 105, 109, 117, 126, 136-137, 162-163, 168, 172-173 (©Jake Rajs 2019)
25, 31, 44-45, 46, 68, 158, 187, 192-193, 200-201, 208 (Paul Seibert courtesy of FlyNYON)
110 (Alan Shortall)
146 (Smithsonian Institution)
147 (Strong Museum of Play, The Iris F. Hollander November Collection)
147 (STUDIOCANAL)
147 (WNBA New York Liberty)
154 (New York View, 2014, © Olimpia Zagnoli. Transit poster commissioned by MTA Arts & Design.)

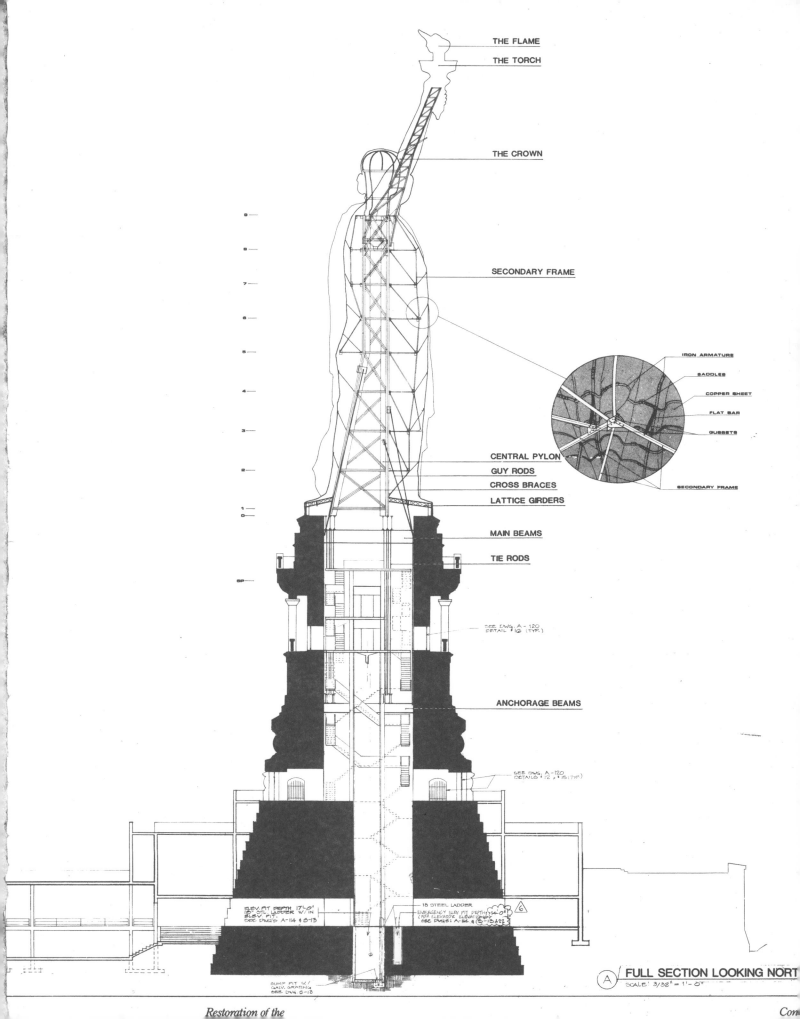

THE FLAME

THE TORCH

THE CROWN

SECONDARY FRAME

IRON ARMATURE

SADDLES

COPPER SHEET

FLAT BAR

GUSSETS

SECONDARY FRAME

CENTRAL PYLON

GUY RODS

CROSS BRACES

LATTICE GIRDERS

MAIN BEAMS

TIE RODS

SEE DWG. A-120
DETAIL #16 (TYP.)

ANCHORAGE BEAMS

SEE DWG. A-120
DETAILS #12 & #15 (TYP.)

ELEV. PIT DEPTH 17'-0"
18" STL LADDER W/IN
ELEV. PIT.
SEE DWG'S A-114 & S-13

18 STEEL LADDER

EMERGENCY ELEV PIT DEPTH 14'-0"
(NEW ELEVATOR ELEVATION)
SEE DWGS: A-114 & S-13A

SUMP PIT W/
GALV. GRATING
SEE DWG S-13

A FULL SECTION LOOKING NORT

SCALE: 3/32" = 1'-0"

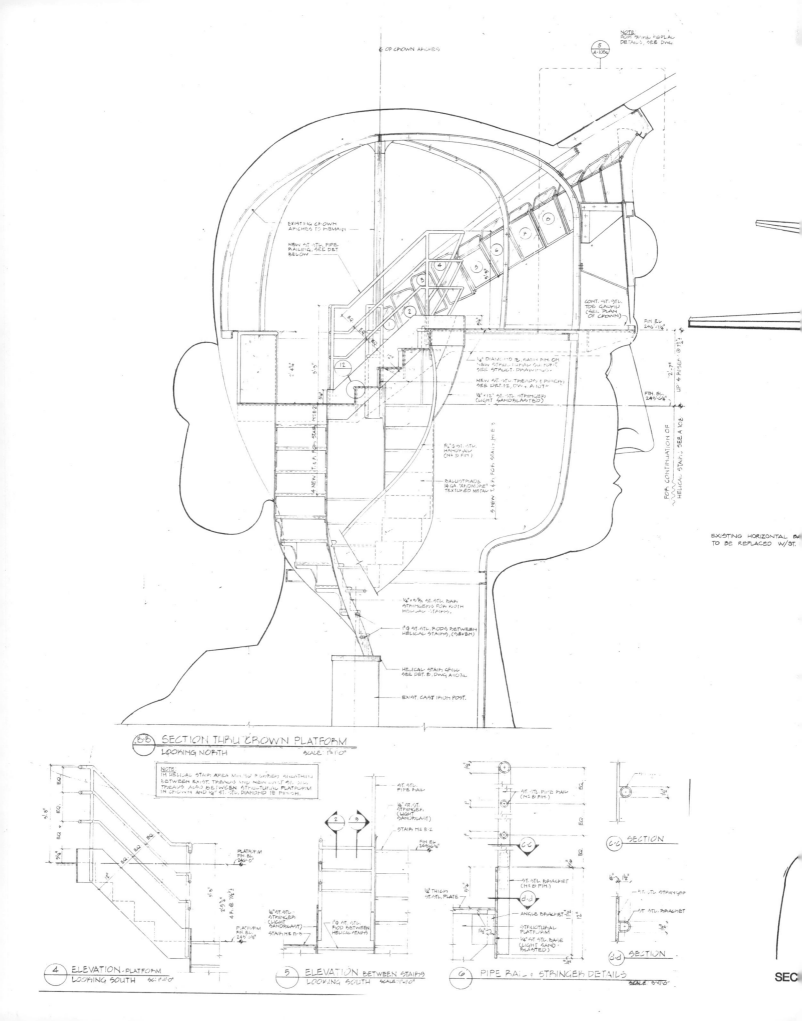